"Good evening. My name is Marty Ackerman. I am thirty-six years old, and I am very rich. I hope to make the Curtis Publishing Company rich—again."

That statement made Martin S. Ackerman famous. In writing about MONEY, EGO, POWER, he isn't merely spouting theory. Ackerman has made it BIG on his own. He has been there, and he has done it all. Now he reveals how you, too, can become rich by being a wheeler-dealer.

In 1962, he bought a small, struggling photofinishing firm called Perfect Photo. Six years later it was Perfect Film and Chemical Corporation, a conglomerate with sales of around $150 million a year. Later Ackerman became president of Curtis Publishing Company. Unfortunately, circumstances forced him to close the ailing **Saturday Evening Post**. But, reports **Dun's Review**, "he succeeded in making Marty Ackerman even richer, partially by selling off some of Curtis's assets—enough to realize a profit of at least double his five-million-dollar investment." Enough, **Dun's** adds, to buy him "four luxurious homes, a Lear jet and walls replete with Picassos and Matisses."

MONEY, EGO, POWER

**MARTIN S. ACKERMAN
& DIANE L. ACKERMAN**

PLAYBOY PRESS
PAPERBACKS

MONEY, EGO, POWER

Copyright © 1976 by Martin S. and Diane L. Ackerman.

All rights reserved. No part of this book may be reproduced, stored in a retrieval system or transmitted in any form by an electronic, mechanical, photocopying, recording means or otherwise without prior written permission of the authors.

Published simultaneously in the United States and Canada by Playboy Press, Chicago, Illinois. Printed in the United States of America. Playboy Press hardcover edition published 1976. Playboy Press softcover edition published 1978.

Books are available at quantity discounts for promotional and industrial use. For further information, write our sales-promotion agency: Ventura Associates, 40 East 49th Street, New York, New York 10017.

ISBN: 0-872-16460-8

For us and our marriage for surviving more than just the writing of this book.

Contents

ACKNOWLEDGMENTS	*xi*
1. Introduction	3
2. So You, Too, Want to Be a Wheeler-Dealer?	6
What Is a Wheeler-Dealer?	6
(Gene Klein; Fred Carr; Arthur Cohen; John Y. Brown; Bert Kleiner; Newt Gleckel; Richard Pistell; Martin Stone; Charles Bluhdorn; Bernard Cornfeld; Kirk Kerkorian; Dr. Norman Orentreich; Art Linkletter; David Frost)	
Money as Motivation	45
Gratifying Your Ego	48
The Gentle Art of Social Climbing	52
Having Fun—and Getting Paid for It	54
Understanding Your Motivations	55
3. Preparing Yourself to Be a Wheeler-Dealer	58
Education	58
Moving in the Right Circles	61
Making Friends and Building Your Team	63

Contents

Selecting the Right Job to Get Started	68
Learn at the Hand of a Master; Finding a Company in Trouble; Help the Old Man Retire; Run with a Fast-Moving Company	
Acquiring a Reputation	71
Establishing Credit	72
Using Paper Money	83
Becoming Chairman of the Board or President	85
Acquiring Equity	90
Watch Your Public Image	91

4. Getting Started — 93

The High Road—or Large Corporations	93
The Low Road—or Small Corporations	99
Your Own Road—or Starting Your Own Corporation	105
Other Roads to Travel	109

5. The Deal Business — 114

Building Your Own Company: Private vs. Public	118
(Howard Hughes—Classic Example of Going Public for the Cash)	
Acquiring a Vehicle	126
Turning Around a Company in Trouble	127
(Herb Engelhardt at Beck; Ackerman at Curtis)	
The Sell-out and the Buy-in	134
(Grassie at Beck)	

Contents

Growth by Merger	*140*
(Vertical Mergers; Horizontal Mergers; The Conglomerate; Concentric)	
Putting a Group Together	*145*
(The Parsons Group)	
Second Man to the Leader	*147*
(Sandy Sigoloff at Republic)	
Jim Slater, Born Wheeler-Dealer	*149*
6. *What Not to Do*	*154*
Jim Ling	*155*
Saul Steinberg	*160*
Glenn W. Turner	*162*
Keith Barrish	*166*
7. *A Four-Point Game Plan*	*169*
The Idea	*169*
Raising the Necessary Funds	*171*
The Use of the Money	*175*
The Capital Structure	*177*
8. *Where Do You Go from Here?*	*179*
9. *Life Style*	*183*
The Best of Everything	*183*
Advice to the Wife	*190*
Sex	*193*
(Marital Sex; Extracurricular Sex; Sex in the Office)	
Staying in Shape	*198*

Contents

10. *Your Future*   200

    Robert Kenmore   201
    Gerry Tsai   202
    The Quiet Life and a Final Warning   203

Acknowledgments

Many people have to be thanked for helping us get this book into print. The original idea for us to write a book came from an old client, Clifford Irving, who obviously longs to be a wheeler-dealer. The discipline and time to sit down and write came from the boredom we encountered when we took a sabbatical from our usual nine-to-five jobs and changed our life style. Editorial assistance and encouragement came from our very talented friend, Gay Search. Our friend and agent Roz Cole deserves the credit for subsequently selling what we wrote. Our extra special thanks also to our longtime associate Cathy Hommel for enduring the typing and retyping of the manuscript; and, to many of our friends, who volunteered their own personal experiences and criticisms. And, finally, to Mike Cohn and his excellent staff at Playboy Press, our sincerest thanks for having the foresight and spirit to publish this book.

MONEY, EGO, POWER

1
Introduction

The wheeler-dealer is the twentieth-century merchant adventurer—or robber baron, depending upon your point of view—a man who rejects the traditional paths and instead hacks out his own shortcut to wealth, power and fame, or maybe, notoriety. He is a supreme opportunist, the ultimate main-chancer, who manipulates money—frequently on paper, and usually other people's—to build or buy and sell companies like Monopoly players buy and sell streets and houses, and who, often, has no interest in what those companies make provided they also make money. His professional activities fill the financial magazines and the business pages, his private life the gossip columns and the pages of many a glossy paperback novel. He is hated by some people, feared by others, but to the vast majority of those who earn their living in the world of business, he is the object of admiration and envy.

MONEY, EGO, POWER

This book is about the wheeler-dealer and his sphere of operation—the deal business—and how, if you have the ambition, the energy and the drive, you too can succeed in it. It takes you step-by-step up the ladder of success, from getting your foot on the first rung—education, motivation, the kind of friends you should make and people you should influence, establishing credit—through climbing the ladder—gaining experience in the right job in the right company, choosing your method of attack and carrying through your first deal—to the top—consolidating your position and staying well and happy while you're up there. It's a book for people who have intelligence, drive and ambition, and while some business sense is a help, a degree from the Harvard Business School isn't a prerequisite for understanding it.

It is also a book for the young entrepreneur, willing to learn and anxious to expand his horizons.

The *Manual for Would-Be Wheeler-Dealers* isn't merely theory, or the fantasy of some middle-aged, middle-manager fending off the realization that he isn't going to make it to the top. I (the senior partner of this writing team) have been there and I've done it! As Kent MacDougall, a former *Wall Street Journal* reporter, recently said, "Marty's deal happy." But, as MacDougall also admitted, I also got out smelling like a rose and making a fistful of money.

Having spent several years in the late 1950s and early 1960s as a corporate lawyer handling deals for other people, I decided to make use of that experience and go into business for myself. In 1962, I bought a small, struggling photofinishing firm called Perfect Photo, which, in

Introduction

six years, became Perfect Film and Chemical Corporation, a conglomerate listed on the New York Stock Exchange whose assets included, at various times, publishing enterprises, film studios, photographic business and mail order entities which grossed around $150 million a year.

Six years later, I became president of the Curtis Publishing Company. Volumes, literally, have been written about my involvement with Curtis Publishing between '68 and '69 and the closing of *The Saturday Evening Post* —much of it untrue or, at least, greatly embellished versions of the truth—and although subsequent developments have proven that many of the unpopular decisions I made then were right, there are valuable lessons to be learned about the deal business from experience; it also goes to show that nobody is perfect. Now, having been a semiretired wheeler-dealer for several years, and working on the theory that the spectator sees most of the game—especially if he happens to be a former player— I want to pass on what I've learned from watching some of the all-time greats like Jim Slater, Meshulam Riklis, Charles Bluhdorn, Larry Tisch, Gene Klein and Saul Steinberg in action, often at very close quarters, and what I've learned the hard way, from firsthand experience. The main point is the all-important risk/gain ratio. Are you willing to take the necessary risks to gain the fame and fortune of the wheeler-dealer? Good luck— maybe you can make it, maybe you can't, but it's fun trying.

2

So You, Too, Want to Be a Wheeler-Dealer?

What Is a Wheeler-Dealer?

For the sake of clarity, perhaps we should define a wheeler-dealer at the outset to avoid confusing him with some of the successful "establishment businessmen" who have achieved their advancement and fame through the classical means of business operation.

The wheeler-dealer is a man or a woman who moves ahead—forges ahead—in his chosen field of endeavor by the most extraordinary means. He takes shortcuts to wealth and success. Not waiting for his turn in line, he pushes ahead with speed, ambition and guts, leaving in his wake the unmistakable impression of flamboyance, even impatience. Often operating just within the existing borders of the laws of finance and morality, he has a unique ability to turn other people's disadvantages into his advantages. What this book is *not* about is those in-

So You, Too, Want to Be a Wheeler-Dealer?

dividuals who go over the line of existing laws and become criminals. Very often, it's hard to tell what is or is not legal by those who look in from the outside. To the many people who regard the wheeler-dealer with disdain, jealousy and even contempt, it's easy to confuse success with dishonesty; but, to anyone who has the training or who has actually been there, there is no confusion—it's either legal or not, and honesty is not a vague moral principle.

Although there are some people who seem to get rich quickly, financial evidence indicates that most of those who eventually make it have traveled a long, hard road that takes a lifetime of work. The average age of millionaires is approximately sixty years, with women slightly younger than men. With this fact in mind and the daily obituary column attesting to the price many men pay for success, the wheeler-dealers have good reason to move ahead as if there were no time to spare. After all, despite the advances of medical science, it is impossible to guarantee longevity or ensure the good health necessary to enjoy success. Certainly, that trip around the world, a ski chalet at Gstaad, the villa in Saint-Jean-Cap-Ferrat and the million-dollar art collection are more enthusiastically and realistically enjoyed by a virile young man who can look ahead to another twenty or thirty years of opulent self-indulgence than by an exhausted sixty-year-old with ulcers and perhaps a heart condition, too.

Just to give you an idea of whom we consider eligible, let's look at a few whose combination of statistics, attitude, impression, flamboyance and personality would, in our opinion, put them into the wheeler-dealer class.

Money, Ego, Power

GENE KLEIN

The story of Eugene Victor Klein, born January 1921 in New York City, is a modern fairy tale in which our hero rose from selling used cars to holding assets worth around a billion dollars in a little over twenty-five years. A very tall, handsome, athletic man with lots of personality and drive, Klein came from a modest background; his father was a small-time clothing manufacturer in New York. After spending three years at the RCA Institute, he joined the Air Force in 1941 as a bomber pilot and left the service five years later as a captain.

Once the war was over, Klein and his wife, Frances, left the East Coast for the land of opportunity, Southern California, and, having borrowed two thousand dollars from his father, he opened his first used-car lot. Now, while people may not have bought used cars from Richard M. Nixon, they bought them from Gene Klein in large numbers. He was a gifted salesman and by the mid-1950s he had made enough money to buy his way into distribution, first of Volkswagens, then of Volvos, at the time when the European invasion of the American automobile market was just beginning.

Cars may have been kind to Klein, but by the beginning of the 1960s he was looking around in other areas for a vehicle of another kind—a company suitable for expansion. He lighted on the National General Corporation, a small public company created in 1952 by Twentieth Century-Fox to handle their movie theaters after a government consent decree had forbidden the compa-

So You, Too, Want to Be a Wheeler-Dealer?

nies that made movies to own the theaters that showed them.

The late 1950s had been a bad time for movie theaters because television was making a huge dent in audience figures. Therefore, Klein was able to buy into the company reasonably cheap. By 1961 he was chief stockholder and a director and in a position to make changes. He realized early that if the audiences were to be lured away from their TV sets and back into the theaters, he must offer them more than just movies. He remodeled the theaters, fought hard for good pictures, and installed large candy counters and hot dog stands in the foyers of his theaters before anyone else caught on to the idea, and they soon became almost his trademark.

The combination of Klein's flair and the financial acumen of his partner, Sam Shulman, a Harvard moneyman, produced a tax loss carry-forward of $11 million—well worth having since, if he could make a profit of $11 million in a similar line of business within a five-year period, that profit would be totally tax free. Having worked a minor miracle with something as seemingly unprofitable as movie theaters, Klein found his borrowing power greatly increased—not only with his local bank, City National Bank of Beverly Hills and its founder, Al Hart, where the fact that he was one of its directors can't have done his chances of getting a loan any harm, but also with the First National Bank of Boston, one of the more adventurous banking operations in America, which was looking to expand its influence to the West Coast.

In 1963, Klein's debt to the banks was $19.9 million. Five years later, it was $124.4 million, a sixfold increase, but the money had been used wisely—to make more money. In 1964, he bought the Columbia Loan and Savings Company, which was later sold at a profit to pay back the First National of Boston. He bought some other small companies, selling them off at a profit, more movie theaters—he even dabbled for a while in movie production by means of an independent production company, but the series of totally unmemorable movies it made lost money so that venture was allowed to die slowly—and then, in 1968, he bought the publishing house of Grosset and Dunlap for $68 million. A big deal for Klein at that time.

But toward the end of the 1960s Klein had reached the same conclusion as Saul Steinberg—that while ventures like movie theaters and publishing made money and were a lot of fun, the ultimate deal was a money deal and that meant banking or insurance. So, with a lot of help from his friends—Arthur Carter, Fred Carr and Bert Kleiner—Klein set his sights on Manhattan's old, conservative Great American Holding Company, whose assets were in insurance and whose coffers were filled with excess cash that had been accumulating over the years.

On paper, the deal didn't look possible. How could a company like National General, with assets of around $125 million, take over a company like Great American Holding with assets of $626 million? But Klein pulled it off and how he did it is the art of wheeling and dealing at its best.

What he did was to issue $400 million worth of Na-

So You, Too, Want to Be a Wheeler-Dealer?

tional General "paper" in the form of convertible debentures which offered Great American's stockholders interest plus the chance to convert the debentures into stock later on, in exchange for the stock they were already holding. Perhaps because Great American had been so conservative and its stockholders felt that the great conglomerate bonanza was passing them by, they accepted Klein's offer—though the role of Bert Kleiner, the flamboyant, hip West Coast stockbroker, in his triumph, shouldn't be underestimated.

Klein wasn't the only wheeler-dealer interested in Great American. Eli Black, then of AMK, another one of the most successful conglomerates of the 1960s, was also in the running, and some commentators believe that if Kleiner hadn't persuaded his clients to throw their support behind Klein, he would never have won the battle. But he did, and having gained total control of Great American, Klein pulled a stroke that has put him in the financial history books.

As the parent company, National General had its partially owned subsidiary, Great American, declare a dividend of $170 million—in cash—$130 million of which ended up in National General's account with the First National of Boston and made National General's stockholders—chief among whom, of course, was Gene Klein himself—very suddenly, stockholders in a very rich, substantial company. From the little league to the big league with one move. In effect, Klein had gotten $170 million in cash in exchange for $400 million in "paper" and, although it wasn't illegal, it was described at the time as "financial rape" and led directly to the New York state legislature changing its laws. These days, it is prohibited for an insurance company to pay a cash dividend to its parent company without the insurance commissioner being informed first.

But Klein's path to the top hasn't been without its minor setbacks, like the $25 million he lost in Minnie Pearl Chicken. It was the brainchild of John Jay Hooker, whose ambitions at the time encompassed not only fried chicken but politics, too, and he was then running for the governorship of Tennessee. He launched Minnie Pearl in 1966 as a rival to Colonel Sanders' Kentucky Fried Chicken, and it was such a success that a new issue of stock was sold through Bert Kleiner's firm, Kleiner, Bell and Company, the most successful stockbrokers on the West Coast. Then, suddenly, the company hit trouble and, although the exact mechanics of the deal are fuzzy, Gene Klein wound up as major backer of Minnie Pearl, losing the whole $25 million he'd invested. At the time, the rumor was that Klein was paying back the favor he owed Kleiner for his help in the battle with AMK over Great American Holding. Twenty-five million dollars isn't, so to speak, chicken feed, but it was by no means catastrophic for Klein or National General. The company had a lot more in the insurance companies—where that came from.

After the Minnie Pearl debacle, it was downhill for National General from then on. The bad market, plus the bad movies, and the high debt to First National of Boston, started Klein on his demise as a major Wall Street figure. Slowly, he started to liquidate to pay off the banks, then he had a fight with his two partners, who

So You, Too, Want to Be a Wheeler-Dealer?

wanted to cash in while they still could, and in the end, in 1974, he sold his stock in National General to another insurance company, which liquidated almost everything but the theaters and the insurance companies. But, have no fear; Klein still must have walked out with tens of millions of dollars—even after paying off all of his personal debts, which were considered sizable.

On the personal side, he had never been the kind of man who simply let his wealth accumulate. He had always lived lavishly and donated large sums to charities and political organizations. True, he did sell his interest in the basketball team—the Seattle Supersonics—but he's hung onto the real toy, the ultimate ego trip for any former college football player, his own football team—the San Diego Chargers. He still travels in style to the airport in the Rolls-Royce that once belonged to Queen Elizabeth. While I am sure he misses the company's Grumman Gulfstream II, a private jet to end all private jets which cost the company $3.5 million to buy and hundreds of thousands to run, I am sure he can charter one if his ego needs it.

But perhaps the real monument to his success—to the art of wheeling and dealing—is his home in Beverly Hills. The house was built by Burton Green, the man who founded Beverly Hills, but the Kleins bought it, not for its own sake, but for its tennis courts. At first they planned to stay in their own home, pulling down Burton Green's house and just using the courts, but that seemed more like owning your own tennis club than having a court in the back yard, so they decided to move in. The house was reduced to a shell and rebuilt inside so that what had been an eight-bedroom mansion became "the biggest two-bedroom house in the world," and it was alleged to have cost Klein over $1.5 million, and several trips to Europe by his wife and her decorator to refurnish it.

The furniture is mainly French and English, from the seventeenth and eighteenth centuries. There's a footbath that belonged to Marie Antoinette, one of the only two in existence; mirrors that belonged to Lord Nelson; a lapis lazuli desk that belonged to a Russian czarina. Yet the paintings are modern, among them works by Picasso, Miró and Modigliani. The resulting style is what one visitor to the house has described as "Beverly Hills Modern"—a style that you just can't duplicate anywhere else in the world. Nevertheless, it is extremely impressive. When Ronald and Nancy Reagan were invited for dinner during his term as governor of California, Mrs. Reagan remarked, "What a wonderful governor's mansion your home would make!" It was with a remark like that, no doubt, that Henry VIII relieved Cardinal Wolsey of *his* home, Hampton Court, but times have changed and the Kleins could afford to take the comment not as a hint but simply as a compliment.

The mark of any top wheeler-dealer is his sense of timing, and Gene Klein's timing, which has always been impeccable, told him not only when to move in but also when to move out, and he is in the happy position now of having quit while he was at the top. Though it's rumored that he's been buying into art recently, he seems to have had his fill of the deal business at a national level.

At fifty-four—twenty-nine years after he started his

So You, Too, Want to Be a Wheeler-Dealer?

used-car lot on borrowed money—Gene Klein still has his Rolls-Royce, his football team, his Beverly Hills palace and an awful lot of money. Not a bad ending for a man with a two-thousand-dollar stake.

FRED CARR

In 1969 Fred Carr was on his way down—although 1967 and 1968 had been great years. The genius behind the Enterprise Fund, with a near $1 billion portfolio, Carr received masses of publicity—especially after his fund ran up a wild 117 percent in 1967 to outpace every other fund in business. It took *Forbes* two years to say, "Frankly, however, we were not terribly impressed." But if *Forbes* wasn't, the rest of the market and certainly all of the would-be wheeler-dealers were.

In the years to come, when the financial history of the 1960s comes to be written, Fred Carr will have a place all to himself. More than anyone else, he has turned the art of investment into a science. When he is thinking of investing in a stock, he examines the company's record and prospects as carefully, as microscopically, as a scientist trying to find a new virus. As he himself put it once, "I realized that you had to approach the market the way porcupines make love—very carefully!"

In 1966, he was invited to become portfolio manager for a new small mutual fund, soon to be known as Enterprise Fund, where he had some $20 million on which to try out his theories. Where Carr differed from everyone else was that he made *all* the decisions himself about which stocks the fund would buy and, rather than concentrating on the high-priced glamour stocks of the time, the IBMs, the Polaroids, the Xeroxes, he decided to back what he called "emerging growth companies"—companies whose stock was then selling at a low price in relation to their earnings and which were in a position to make the most of their potential.

Not surprisingly, it was to Fred Carr that a good many wheeler-dealers looked. Many funds would not even look at their stock, but Carr would, if you could convince him that yours was about to become "hot." No doubt about it, if it hadn't been for Carr, then Bert Kleiner, Saul Steinberg and Gene Klein may well not have made the big time. That's not to say, though, that Fred Carr was a gambler—anyone controlling investments in a fund that can run up a staggering 117 percent, as Enterprise did in 1967, needs considerably more than luck.

During the late 1960s Carr was the golden boy. When Enterprise's parent company, Shareholders' Capital, went public in late 1968, people were lining up to buy its stock, but success can bring its own problems. When the market started to slump in 1970, Enterprise had grown so large that it had lost a good deal of the flexibility that it needed if it was going to ride out the storm, and Carr's own success had resulted in his being promoted into a position where he had less control over the fund's investments—what had made Enterprise great in the first place.

In 1970, Carr left Enterprise and set up his own company, Fred Carr Associates, managing money for individuals and institutions and providing a financial con-

So You, Too, Want to Be a Wheeler-Dealer?

sultation service for companies of all sizes. Quietly, Fred Carr is already on the way back up, and when the market really turns, he'll be a man to watch, and, this time, at least some of the money he will be investing will be his own.

ARTHUR COHEN

Arthur Cohen, chief executive of Arlen Realty and Development, is one of the few wheeler-dealers to have made his money initially from real estate. His father, a Brooklyn lawyer, was a small-time investor in real estate, and Arthur Cohen's fascination with it goes back to childhood days, but when he came to put that interest into practice there were no extensive family funds to give him his break.

With hindsight, he says it was the best thing that could have happened to him—since he had no money of his own to invest, it made no difference to him whether a deal cost $250,000 or $250 million. In both cases, he had to set about raising the money from other people. The secret of Cohen's success in real estate is really very simple. Select properties with potential for a rapid increase in value, and whenever humanly possible use other people's money. He makes a point of investing nothing but his energy and creativity—"sweat equity," it's sometimes called—or as little of his own money as he can possibly get away with.

His first real estate venture—building VA and FHA-financed housing in Huntington, Long Island, with two partners—meant having to scrape together $25,000, but he made $100,000 on the venture. After that, he set up Arlen, and by investing in real estate and land in Yonkers and in Florida, he made his first million in less than a year. By 1960, by branching out into building luxury apartments, small office buildings and shopping centers, which were to become Arlen's trademark, his own stake in his real estate holdings was $5 million.

Although Arlen built the prestigious Olympic Tower in New York City, Cohen has always known that "bread and butter" building, like shopping centers, was where the real money was, providing what he calls a "hard base of income"—rents from the stores—and some kind of hedge against inflation since he always tries to retain ownership of the land so that he will reap the benefits of any future appreciation.

Now, Arlen and all its subsidiaries, including Spartans Industries, which belonged to Cohen's father-in-law, Charles Bassine, before the merger in 1971, and the bedeviled USIF Real Estate, the offshore real estate fund whose problems contributed in no small part to the collapse of Gramco, is worth billions of dollars. (See chapter 6 under "Keith Barrish.") In spite of that, Wall Street is still wary of Arlen, as it is of most public real estate companies, and the performance of its stock has been disappointing. Cohen himself is not worried. His personal fortune is estimated to be around $200 million—not a bad return on that original $25,000 stake.

So You, Too, Want to Be a Wheeler-Dealer?

JOHN Y. BROWN

Like almost all wheeler-dealers, John Y. Brown, the mastermind behind the astronomical success of Colonel Sanders' Kentucky Fried Chicken, is a man who really likes to work. While he was at law school, he took a job selling the *Encyclopaedia Britannica* in his spare time, even though his father could have supported him. By the time he graduated he was already a district manager with a team of thirty salesmen working for him.

Having turned down an offer to become a regional manager for Britannica, he went to work in his father's law practice. Legal training can be one of the most important assets a would-be wheeler-dealer can acquire. In John Y. Brown's case, his professional training brought him into contact with one Colonel Sanders, who, at that time, was supplying some six hundred restaurants in the United States and Canada with his "unique blend of herbs and spices" from his own home, and at four cents for every chicken sold was making a cool $300,000 a year.

John Y. Brown not only had the insight to realize the potential in the rapidly growing fast-food market for Kentucky Fried Chicken but had the courage to back his belief by raising a $160,000 loan and dedicating himself to getting the company off the ground by working twenty-four hours a day, seven days a week if he had to. With backing from financier Jack Massey, Brown bought the Colonel out for $2 million and worked for six months without any salary, crisscrossing the country to pull the franchise together.

Colonel Sanders' Kentucky Fried Chicken turned out to lay golden eggs, not only for Brown, whose stock at one point in 1969 was worth some $60 million, but for over a hundred fifty people who became millionaires as a result of their investment in Kentucky Fried Chicken, including Massey, who made some $35 million, and Brown's secretary, who turned a stake of $5,000 into $3 million. In 1970, Kentucky Fried Chicken was hit, like everything else, by the recession, and when it merged with Heublein, Inc., in 1971, Brown's holdings were worth a mere $31 million!

Still in his early forties, Brown can now enjoy the fruits of a short but very intense period of labor, but, with his passion for activity, that does not mean a life of idleness. He has political ambitions, and it will certainly be interesting to see if he can do for American politics what he did for fried chicken.

BERT KLEINER

There are very few people who have met Bert Kleiner and haven't liked him. For a while, Kleiner was without doubt *the* most successful stockbroker in America, and yet he doesn't even get a mention in Chris Welles's new book, *The Last Days of the Club*. *Sic transit gloria financial mundi.*

Anyone who read the financial news could not fail to be aware of Bert Kleiner, the forty-seven-year-old former Beverly Hills stockbroker and former corporate deal-maker. He wore long sideburns, which were clipped

So You, Too, Want to Be a Wheeler-Dealer?

in an old-fashioned barber's chair in his office, collected modern art, patronized movements of all kinds, tooled around town in a souped-up Excalibur automobile honking at his show-biz friends in Beverly Hills, and jetted back and forth across the country looking into one deal after another.

Was this any way for a financier to act, *Forbes* asked. Perhaps not, but it is money and accomplishments, not style, that ultimately command respect, and, during the late 1960s, Bert Kleiner had more than his fair share of both. Just eighteen years ago, he was a customers' man at the Los Angeles firm of Cantor, Fitzgerald & Co., the same Bernie Cantor who helped Meshulam Riklis. In 1961, he teamed with fellow customers' man Lionel Bell and Hollywood lawyer Ralph Shapiro to start the firm of Kleiner, Bell and Company with capital of $350,000. In 1968, their original investment had grown to over $60 million in assets and around $10 million in net worth. Most of the growth, and the collapse that was to follow, came as a result of Kleiner's own activities as a dealmaker. Kleiner, Bell was one of the 1960s' most aggressive deal-making firms, earning their commissions as a result of mergers, acquisitions, tender offers, and taking new companies public. Unlike the older, more established New York investment bankers, Bert Kleiner never relied on commission income from trades, but looked instead to the wheeler-dealers as his customers. Kleiner's flamboyant ways were a handicap in the East, especially with the New York Stock Exchange. Not so in the West.

Today, Bert Kleiner is gone—out of the securities business forever. "I won't go back into that jungle," he has said. "Make one mistake and they try to get you." Of course, he made more than one mistake—but his career was extraordinary. Many of those he helped—Gene Klein at National General and Harris Aston at General Host, for example—owe everything to Bert Kleiner and his winning ways. I don't think he will ever be back in the deal business, but if you get the chance to talk to him for an hour or two, you will understand exactly what being a wheeler-dealer is all about.

NEWT GLECKEL

By deciding to sell Hygrade, we assume that Newt Gleckel is calling it a day. Brooklyn-born Newton Gleckel was something of a corporate jack-of-all-trades. He started out as a lawyer, later became a book publisher, a real estate speculator, and the head of an insulation company.

Finally, in 1955, when he was forty, Gleckel took over a troubled Indiana auto-body maker and in less than a decade transformed it into Divco-Wayne Industries. By then, however, he was getting restless again. He sold out to Boise Cascade, getting $22 million in Boise common stock for his interest. Then, he invested in an afternoon tabloid, the *New York Daily Column,* and spent $3 million to buy control of A. S. Beck. He perished, financially, in the attempt. It was one of the few deal companies to go into bankruptcy. (See chapter 7 under "Raising the Necessary Funds.")

Gleckel still lives in a lavish apartment on Park Avenue

and eats lunch at fashionable Manhattan restaurants like "21." To be sure, he has taken a sharp paper loss, at least in Beck, but he's still living high, mainly from his profits at Hygrade Foods, a company on the American Stock Exchange.

RICHARD PISTELL

Richard Pistell was the boss of General Host for a few years. He made one big mistake—going for control of Armour & Company. When Pistell made his move, General Host had a net worth of about $38 million. Then, it went after Armour, a company at least four times its size and controlled by conservative midwesterners. The Armour management, having discouraged Gulf + Western, thought that it could easily defeat Richard Pistell and his wheeler-dealer allies. Pistell, however, accepted the challenge and bought a big block of stock from Charles Bluhdorn's Gulf + Western, more on the open market and even more in a tender offer. And what a tender offer it was. Ask Bert Kleiner, or Herbie Allen, Jr.

General Host ended up with 57 percent of Armour—and it wasn't enough. Armour & Company ended up with Chicago's Greyhound Corporation, and Pistell was out. He probably left by choice, but the pressures must have been great. It was said at that time that he had had enough of the rough and tumble. And who could blame him?

There is no doubt that the General Host tender deal put Bert Kleiner out of business, and plenty of his customers lost a bundle, along with customers of Allen & Company. But, if you will look at Pistell's second man, ex-Yale tackle, lawyer Harris J. Aston, you will see a new kind of wheeler-dealer, who is beginning to revive the company.

MARTIN STONE

Martin Stone, the founder of Los Angeles's Monogram Industries, must be giving a lot of thought these days to the perils of diversification for, as *Forbes* has said, if his $140 million (sales) company had not diversified, it could be riding high as one of the country's most profitable small companies.

Monogram is a leading manufacturer of self-contained recirculating toilets, which it started selling to the commercial aircraft industry and now sells to pleasure boats, travel trailers, construction sites—to any place that needs to, or must by law, replace the outhouse. New and stringent antipollution laws in many states make the prospects in this market even brighter.

But Monogram no longer shines as a growth stock—at last look it traded around 12 7/8, some seven times earnings, down from its high of 81 in the 1960s.

The trouble was that Stone decided to make Monogram a conglomerate. Monogram already had something of a conglomerate mix when Stone took command in 1961, but he streamlined the company by concentrating on its toilet business. Having done that successfully, he started to diversify and pushed his earnings up by acquir-

So You, Too, Want to Be a Wheeler-Dealer?

ing a supplier of insulating materials to the electronics industry, a $38-million-a-year-sales producer of industrial screws, and a wire and cable supplier to the computer industry. The fastener business was his biggest problem in 1970.

The acquisitions soon sent sales figures soaring, but they submerged Monogram's good little toilet business. In the 1960s, of course, conglomerates were the rage, and since Monogram commanded a 30-to-40-times earnings ratio, which made acquisitions easier to make, there seemed no reason to stop acquiring still more companies. Stone's press agents were proclaiming him as the "next Tex Thornton," and *Business Week* thought he might be a candidate for governor of the state of California. But Stone soon began to find, like many other conglomerateurs, that acquiring companies meant acquiring problems, and Stone is trying to work his way out.

CHARLES BLUHDORN

If we had to pick the man whose accomplishments and personality make him Mr. American wheeler-dealer of all time, we would pick Charles Bluhdorn. Bluhdorn started in the commodity market, a refugee from Europe. He was a millionaire in his mid-twenties, but that didn't stop him from trying to make it even bigger.

First, he welded together a solid component manufacturing complex and distribution system for his auto parts business out of Texas. Between 1958 and 1965, his sales moved from $8 million to $182 million, but all in auto parts. The big one was New Jersey Zinc in February 1966. This really marked Gulf + Western as an emerging conglomerate. Like the rest of his breed, Bluhdorn understood the leveraging of capital with high borrowings. And, it worked—and formed the base for Paramount, E. W. Bliss, Universal American, Consolidated Cigar, and so on, and so on, and so on. . . .

Gulf + Western's profits for 1976 are expected, on the results of the first two quarters, to exceed $207.5 million, an increase of almost 30 percent on the record profits of the previous year. Looking at Gulf + Western's figures, you have to remind yourself that this is supposed to be an extremely tough time, economically. And you know that Charlie Bluhdorn will gain a great deal of pleasure from those results.

Fortune, in March 1968, said of the man, "He delights in the scale of his dealings. His manner changes swiftly from persuasive explanation to table-thumping assertion, all enunciated in mile-a-minute Viennese-American. His single-mindedness about the rightness and logic of his mission in the business world can display itself in rudeness and irascibility, as well as in sudden charm." Once he has you cornered in a room in order to make the deal, he usually succeeds. I know. I have been so cornered. Most of the people who know him and who have done business with him have admiration for Bluhdorn that borders on love. He made his mistakes, like most of us, but he has also learned to listen as well as talk, and the Charles Bluhdorn of 1976 almost looks and acts like he will soon be admitted to the Union League Club—in New York, that is. Philadelphia will take a little longer.

So You, Too, Want to Be a Wheeler-Dealer?

BERNARD CORNFELD

What is there left to be said about Bernard Cornfeld? Very little, you might think, but for a man whose life, for years, was chronicled in detail by the press, old habits die hard, and he can still be relied upon to come up with a good story. The most recent report is that he is about to have his first child—or, rather, the lady in his life is about to have his first child, though, knowing Cornfeld, nothing would actually surprise us.

Perhaps because he ran into serious trouble, and spent some time as a nonpaying guest of the Swiss government (and it looks like he will also do the same in the United States), more has been written about Bernie Cornfeld than almost any other wheeler-dealer around. We know that he was born in Turkey in 1927 to Jewish parents from central Europe and came to America—Brooklyn— when he was a child. His father, a theatrical promoter and actor, died when he was very young, and his mother has been his great friend and loyal supporter throughout his life.

He graduated from high school with a B-plus average and served in the U.S. Merchant Marine during the Second World War. When he left the service, he went to Brooklyn College, where, according to a college acquaintance, he was a "reform-the-world nut" and had no time for capitalism and its fruits. He came out with a B.S. degree in psychology and, having drifted through a number of minor jobs, ended up as a youth counselor in Philadelphia, where he stayed until 1954. For no particular, compelling reason, he left Philadelphia and moved to New York City, where he took a job as a mutual fund salesman. In the 1950s, a time when mutual funds were doing a roaring business, it was a job that needed no qualifications and very little skill, apart from the ability to speak English and smile at the relevant points in the spiel. In those days, too, mutual funds seemed like the answer to every small investor's prayer, so it wasn't difficult for a mutual fund salesman to make money, and Bernie Cornfeld did pretty well for an average young American of the period.

Looking for a change of environment, and still a bachelor, he decided to go to Europe to see whether it was still as he remembered it from his Merchant Marine days. So, in 1955 he went to Paris, with his company's blessing though at his own expense, to see whether he could sell mutual fund shares to the Europeans—and Europe has never been the same since. In one sense, Bernie Cornfeld was a modern-day Gertrude Stein, though it's unlikely that either party would be particularly flattered by the comparison. Both were drawn to Europe, to Paris in particular, by its untapped potential, though in Gertrude Stein's case, it was art, while in Cornfeld's, it was money.

European governments did not exactly welcome him with open arms—their economies were still struggling to recover from the devastation of the war, and they did not want to see their precious capital being drained off to be invested in healthy, booming American companies. So Cornfeld was forbidden to sell to their citizens, but, not daunted, he turned his attention to the large numbers of American servicemen, diplomats and businessmen living and working in Europe. In those days, an American pay-

So You, Too, Want to Be a Wheeler-Dealer?

check went a long way in Europe, and there was almost always plenty left over at the end of each month, but while the expatriates could read in the European editions of their newspapers of the boom at home, there was no way, unless they were able to make the transatlantic crossing frequently, to instruct their brokers so that they could take part in it.

And then along came Bernie Cornfeld, offering them the opportunity to invest, indirectly, in American industry, and, not surprisingly, the money began to pour in.

In America, mutual funds were well established, and thousands of salesmen made a reasonably good living from persuading people to invest in them. In Europe, when Cornfeld arrived, hardly anybody had heard about mutual funds; they were sold through the banks, like any other stocks, not by men who sat in your living room and painted a glorious financial future for you over a cup of coffee. Cornfeld realized the potential and was extremely well rewarded for that one stroke of insight. Investors' Overseas Service—or "I.O.S.," letters which became as famous as ITT or CBS—was established in Switzerland in the late 1950s as the European outlet for an established American fund, Dreyfus & Company, and the original I.O.S. sales team was small enough to fit into Cornfeld's far-from-capacious car.

Cornfeld became the great and legendary salesman. Cornfeld, the American upstart, was the American to be reckoned with in Europe in the late 1950s and the 1960s. The press covered his every success, both personal and financial. Those who started with him and were part of the initial Cornfeld enterprise were considered the most successful Americans in Europe, although most of them were in Europe as washouts of one kind or another. The story of Bernie Cornfeld, as told in the European newspapers, became as often told as the story of John D. Rockefeller. It was the traditional American story of rags to riches.

Soon Cornfeld was able to start his own mutual fund —International Investment Trust—incorporated in Luxembourg, where the financial laws, to say the least, are pretty unrestricting. Within a year, it had collected over $3.5 million of other people's money—no mean sum, and yet peanuts compared to the *billion and a half dollars* which the fund controlled at its peak.

To most Americans in the finance business, especially those in the up-and-coming brokerage firms on Wall Street, dealing with Bernie Cornfeld seemed like the road to instant success. Just knowing him gave you a head start. Of course, the reasoning was easy to understand. With Cornfeld controlling all that money, if you got to know him, maybe he would put some of it your way, legitimately, of course. If. I.O.S. liked your company, they could become (through the funds they controlled) a major purchaser of your stock in the open market. And if that happened, the price went up. If you were really close to Bernie, maybe you could sell some of your unregistered stock to one of the funds at a discount from market. Convertible debentures, outright loans, all of these things meant money—and plenty of it. At one time or another, Cornfeld was in everything—in most of the "hot" stocks of the 1960s on Wall Street.

So You, Too, Want to Be a Wheeler-Dealer?

They lent glamour to I.O.S.—its investors felt that they were really "in" on the boom, and as long as their stock was making money, it didn't matter that Bernie Cornfeld was making a fortune out of it, too.

Everybody with a deal wanted to show it to Cornfeld, but, in that sense, he was rather like the Wizard of Oz—once you reached him, you knew he would be able to grant most of your financial wishes, but reaching him made the Yellow Brick Road look like an open doorway to the Wizard's Palace. It was said that certain brokers, like Oppenheimer & Company, or Fred Alger, were close to I.O.S. money and Cornfeld, so some people tried that way. Other people found the only way was through the late Bobby Feldman, Cornfeld's regular tennis opponent, or through Claude Giroux, one of Cornfeld's personal friends. Other approaches were comparatively direct. Bert Kleiner, for Commonwealth United, for example, simply went through Barry Sterling, a lawyer friend who was "the lawyer" and a member of the I.O.S. board of directors.

The approach was always haphazard, and any examination of the I.O.S. mutual fund portfolios would have revealed, we suspect, a story behind every stock and each convertible note in which the fund invested, and a connection somewhere. Large fees were undoubtedly earned by many who had unraveled, and who understood, the way to Cornfeld kingdom.

It is hard to write anything about Cornfeld without writing a whole book, but, in his way, he was the prince of the kingdom, certainly in Europe, if not the prince *in absentia* in America. He had what everyone else wanted—money and position—and his looked like the ultimate success story.

His life style was unequaled by any wheeler-dealer in the United States, with the exception of Hugh Hefner. He was the presidents' president, the wheeler-dealers' wheeler-dealer. He had a chateau in Switzerland and a great, expensively decorated apartment in Paris, townhouses in London and in New York. He traveled on his own airplane—an airplane like no one else, Hefner, Kerkorian included, could afford. He owned his own tailoring company, for his special designs. He wore custommade French suits and Italian shoes in the latest styles—an indulgence more than anything else since nature had decreed that Bernie Cornfeld, no matter how much money he spent, would never look elegant. He opened his own New York delicatessen in Geneva so he wouldn't miss his hot pastrami and cold corned beef. He affected a small, tufty beard when he thought he had to look more like an established European businessman. He traveled everywhere with a convoy of beautiful girls of sundry nationalities, most of them ten or twenty years younger than he. He picked up every check, went to every party and was where you expected all of the "beautiful people" to be. He would turn up at such jet-setting watering spots as Acapulco, Mexico, and make headlines simply by arriving. Photographers would scramble to take leggy pictures of the famous miniskirt platoon with which he traveled. He was covered in *Life*, *Look* and *The New Yorker*. Until Bernard Cornfeld, people had always expected financiers to be quiet, sober and prudent. But here was

So You, Too, Want to Be a Wheeler-Dealer?

an international swinger who controlled millions of other peoples' money. Many people in the financial world didn't like it; Cornfeld, they felt, was giving the staid, traditional world of money a bad name. But, undoubtedly, he was the man of his time.

Trouble began in the late 1960s, when some of the less prudent fund speculations turned sour. It wasn't serious trouble at first, but it was aggravated by some internal management and cost problems—by sheer mismanagement, unhappy shareholders were to allege later—and resulted in an acute shortage of cash.

In 1969, I.O.S. went public. It certainly helped Cornfeld and many of his team to get some cash out—they were able to sell some of their shares in the company on the open market at a time when it would have been almost impossible to find a buyer privately and come away with cash—but it did little for I.O.S. itself. By 1970, the company was in real trouble, so a group of directors and major shareholders got together and picked Bernie Cornfeld as the scapegoat. He was voted out of the company he founded. He made several attempts to regain control, but they all failed.

What went wrong is legendary; why it went wrong is another story. Cornfeld was what was wrong with I.O.S. He could never live up to his press notices; I.O.S. could never be as successful as it was said to be. Trying to be a financial superstar when he was really just another wheeler-dealer was what ultimately destroyed I.O.S. and, we think, Cornfeld.

The money and possessions became secondary, after a while, to the quest for power and position. Cornfeld abdicated his responsibilities to others in areas that he knew little about, but, even so, they acted not in their own name (for Bernie was always in real control during this period) but in Bernie's name, because they thought this was the way he wanted it. And they were right—he did want it that way, because they told him this was the shortcut to the top, the unassailable pinnacle, the way to become so big that he would be beyond attack.

He was starting to believe he was a prince among princes. When things began to go wrong, his associates could not face their failures—if they had, it's possible that the whole empire could have been saved. Instead, they tried to hide its true position from him, because they knew that his ego could not stand defeat.

The Cornfeld story is unique in that Bernie Cornfeld operated, not in America, where we have full disclosure, but abroad, where, even with the best informal network of information, it was possible for him to cloak almost everything he did with mystery. When things went bad, everybody suspected the worst—and maybe they had a right to, for mystery and suspicion were the trademarks of Cornfeld's way of operating.

KIRK KERKORIAN

At the other end of the spectrum is Kirk Kerkorian, the dropout kid who made good. Whatever else Kirk Kerkorian is, he is a survivor, a man who has proved that he can pull himself back from the brink of total catastrophe and not merely survive, but flourish.

So You, Too, Want to Be a Wheeler-Dealer?

In many ways, Kerkorian, a fifty-nine-year-old Armenian wheeler-dealer, seems very like the late Howard Hughes. Both men had considerable interests in aviation, movies and Las Vegas and both have a strong dislike of public occasions, but, although Kerkorian has incurred the wrath of Metro-Goldwyn-Mayer stockholders by rarely if ever appearing at stockholders' meetings, he is by no means the total recluse that Hughes became in the last years of his life.

Their origins, though, could hardly have been more different. Hughes had a head start in that his father had already built a considerable family fortune, whereas Kerkorian's father was an unsuccessful wheeler-dealer and Kerker—or Kirk, as he became known—spent his childhood moving from home to home whenever yet another of his father's ventures failed. From a very early age, he helped supplement the family's income by selling newspapers or caddying at the local golf course (perhaps one good reason why golf, a traditional businessman's sport, never appealed to him). Schooling was a luxury the Kerkorians could hardly afford, and Kirk dropped out in the eighth grade. It was the depression, though, and work was hard to come by so he joined the Civilian Conservation Corps when he was seventeen by lying about his age.

In 1939, he went up in an airplane for the first time, a joy ride that changed his life. He decided to learn to fly, and lacking the money to pay for tuition, he milked cows and worked on a range in exchange for lessons. In 1941, although he lacked the two years' college then necessary to join an air academy as an instructor, he was taken on at Morton, with the help of a fake high school degree. When America entered the war, he joined the Royal Air Force to ferry lend-lease bombers across the Atlantic to England—an extremely dangerous occupation since flying across the Atlantic was still comparatively untried.

Once the war was over, he used his wartime savings to buy an old DC-3 and began flying freight all over the country. In 1947, he bought Los Angeles Air Services and built up a business, not only buying and selling ex-service airplanes, but also operating a nonschedule charter service. After the war, there were hundreds of "nonsched" companies like Kerkorian's, run by ex-service pilots using ex-service planes, but he and Bob Prescott were the only two to survive in that business.

From early on, Kerkorian showed the flair and the sense of timing that are essential qualities for any would-be wheeler-dealer. He learned quickly, for example, that if he used the planes he bought to sell, then he could take depreciation on them while he was using them, and then, when he did sell, he could sell as capital gains and pay a lower rate of tax than if he had simply sold them straight off. Because he *knew* airplanes, he knew exactly what he was buying—like the DC-4 freighter he bought and refitted as a passenger airliner for less than $100,000 (the first of many sizable loans made to him by the Montebello branch of the Bank of America) when the going rate for a secondhand passenger DC-4 was $150,000, and sold two years later for $340,000.

And because he knew airplanes, he had an instinct for the way the aviation business was moving. When the Civil Aeronautics Board placed severe restrictions on the

So You, Too, Want to Be a Wheeler-Dealer?

nonscheds in the early 1950s, Kerkorian had already divided the business into two—*he* bought planes and leased them to LAAS, so that when they had to stop flying, he was able to carry on buying and selling planes, many of which he picked up at bargain-basement prices from other nonscheds forced out of business.

Kerkorian was also one of the first to realize the potential of government contract work for charter aircraft, and also of jets when they were introduced to commercial service in the late 1950s. In 1962, Trans International Airlines (what Los Angeles Air Services had become in 1960 when Kerkorian felt the original name was too parochial) bought a DC-8, and, later that year, Kerkorian sold the company to Studebaker in exchange for $1 million's worth of their stock, though he still operated TIA. Nineteen sixty-three was a memorable year for Kerkorian. He leased his jet to the Los Angeles Lodge of the Odd Fellows and thereby launched what was to become the biggest boom air travel had ever known—the cheap group affinity charter. He also bought a piece of real estate in Las Vegas. He liked the place—it had sentimental significance since many of his early charters had been to fly gamblers and honeymooners out there, and in those days he had also liked to gamble. In 1950, he had made his first investment in the Nevada gold mine—$50,000 in the Sands Hotel—and had lost the lot. He vowed then never to invest another nickel in any business of which he did not have control.

And in 1963, he no longer controlled TIA and it was a situation he didn't like, so he began to sell his Studebaker stock to raise the money he needed to buy his company back. Studebaker wanted $2.5 million for it. Kerkorian raised a $2 million loan from his friendly neighborhood Bank of America, found the other half million himself and, in 1964, not only bought back his company but went public, and by selling only 23 percent of the stock, raised enough to pay off the bank loan and cover his own investment. When he finally sold out again in 1968, to Transamerica Corporation, TIA was worth $150 million, of which $85 million went to Tracy Investment Company, the company he had set up in 1959 to handle his personal finances, and named after his first daughter.

In the meantime, his interests in Las Vegas were growing. A hotel—Caesars Palace—was built in 1966 on the piece of land he had bought for less than $1 million, and it brought in around $2 million annually in rent. In 1967, he bought the famous—or maybe "notorious" is more accurate—Flamingo Hotel and another piece of land on which he planned to build the International Hotel. The mid-1960s period, of course, was the peak of Howard Hughes's activities, and, ignoring the fact that Kerkorian had been there first, Hughes made several attempts to block Kerkorian's Las Vegas operation. Kerkorian's request to the Bank of America for a $60 million loan to finance the building of the International Hotel was turned down, while a request for a $75 million loan to buy Western Airlines stock was granted only a few months later on the strength of Kerkorian's signature alone. It was rumored at the time that the fact that Hughes was one of the Bank of America's biggest depositors was not a total coincidence.

So You, Too, Want to Be a Wheeler-Dealer?

In 1969, the International Leisure Corporation, which controlled both the International and the Flamingo hotels, went public and 17 percent of the stock raised $26.5 million. Kerkorian not only owned the controlling interest in that company, but he also had a controlling interest in Western Air Lines and, in June 1968, having sold off his shares in Transamerica for $68 million, he was able to pay back the bulk of the loan from Bank of America, with which he'd bought his Western stock, and make a bid for control of the ailing Metro-Goldwyn-Mayer. Edgar Bronfman, then in control of MGM, was not prepared to let Kerkorian take over without a struggle. He fought him in the courts on the grounds that Kerkorian was planning to finance the deal with a loan from Transamerica Finance Corporation, a subsidiary of Transamerica, but since they owned a controlling interest in United Artists, there was the possibility of a violation of the antitrust laws. Nothing if not flexible, Kerkorian changed his plans and, instead, flew to Europe, where he raised some $72 million, offering, as collateral, assets worth 150 percent of that amount.

At the end of 1969, such a situation posed no threat to Kerkorian, a man worth somewhere in the region of a quarter of a *billion* dollars. But, for him, as for thousands of investors, big and small, 1970 was to change the situation disastrously. In Kerkorian's case, it wasn't merely the world slump that pushed him toward the brink of financial disaster. The Securities and Exchange Commission also lent a hand. Early in 1970, he planned to make a secondary offering of International Leisure shares to raise $28.5 million to repay part of the European loan which was coming due, but the Securities and Exchange Commission refused to grant permission on the grounds that Kerkorian had failed to declare certain irregularities in the operations of the Flamingo's casino, in the bad old days before he took over. What the SEC was saying, in effect, was that unless Kerkorian could produce the old regime's books, then it would not permit any further issue of stock.

Kerkorian is a realist and recognizes the impossible when he sees it. The only course of action open to him was to sell International Leisure. It could not have happened at a worse time. The recession had begun to hit hard—stock prices were way down and interest rates were way up. Many companies, including Western, International, Leisure and MGM, had to forego paying any dividends at all that year.

All Kerkorian's possessions were technically up for sale: his house in Las Vegas, his $1 million yacht, and his pride and joy—his personal plane. Summer 1970 was nail-biting time for Kerkorian. His foreign loan amounted to around $72 million, so the 150 percent collateral he had to put up had to be worth around $100 million or his creditors had the right to call in the loan at any time, and it was estimated that his holdings in the three companies, at the bottom of the market, were only worth about $90 million. Many people in Kerkorian's position would have panicked, and yet his biographer, Dial Torgerson, reports that Kerkorian would ring stockbroker friends and ask amiably if any of his broker friends had jumped out of the window yet, as though the whole crisis was having no effect on him personally at all.

So You, Too, Want to Be a Wheeler-Dealer?

Kerkorian's iron nerve carried him through, though. He managed to persuade one of his European creditors to extend the loan and, by selling half his interest in International Leisure to the Hilton organization for $16.5 million (a real bargain for Hilton since a half share the year before had been worth around $80 million), was able to pay off the other creditor.

Over the next year, he sold the rest of his holding in International Leisure to Hilton and paid off the rest of his European loan. Admittedly, he made a profit on the Las Vegas interlude of some $33 million, but it was nowhere near as much as it should have been. Kerkorian was out of Las Vegas again, but not for long.

Over the next few years, he gradually sold off his stock in Western Airlines and invested the money in more MGM stock. Under his control, the company diversified —often in the face of vociferous opposition from some stockholders. The unprofitable movie-making operation was gradually dismantled and sold off to companies like United Artists and CIC, and MGM's pride and joy now is the MGM Grand Hotel—a multimillion-dollar exercise in nostalgia which opened in Las Vegas (where else?) in 1973.

In January 1976, it was announced that Kerkorian planned to sell what remaining Western stock he had so that he could concentrate full-time on MGM. It was rumored that he also wanted the money to pay off part of MGM's debt to the Bank of America. So, once again, all Kerkorian's eggs are in one basket, but he has made it work before and there is no reason why he shouldn't do it again. He is a survivor, and as one colleague put it, he has "balls of steel." But what nobody seems too sure about is what his prime motivation is. What makes Kirk run? It's certainly not the need to maintain a lavish life style; he and his family live modestly by multimillionaire standards. He's never owned a Rolls-Royce but has made do with a Firebird, and the plane, his one real luxury, was sold some years ago to Adnan Mohammed Khashoggi, a Saudi Arabian businessman and financier. It's certainly not the thrill of the board-room struggle; Kerkorian gets restless after half an hour and needs to stretch his legs, and that is assuming he's turned up in the first place. And it seems unlikely that it's the need for security; if that's your motivation, you don't lay everything you own on the line, as he has done more than once. Kerkorian remains, among wheeler-dealers, something of a mystery man, but, in the end, he may turn out to be as successful, and as much of a "stayer," as Larry Tisch.

The impression you have probably gained from what you have read so far is that wheeler-dealers are all in the business of business. Not so. It's a profession open to all; doctors, television personalities, fashion designers can also make a killing.

DR. NORMAN ORENTREICH

Unlike Dr. Harold Land, founder and inventor of the Polaroid camera, Dr. Norman Orentreich is a medical doctor. The financial worth of his practice might not be

So You, Too, Want to Be a Wheeler-Dealer?

nearly so staggering as that of the professional doctors, but the scope of what he has done within the medical profession ranks him among the wheeler-dealers.

As head of the Orentreich Medical Group, which currently includes two other dermatologists besides himself, he maintains an office on Fifth Avenue that consists of three doctors, fifteen registered nurses, ten receptionists, sixteen rooms, two floors and seven hundred patients per week with skin problems. Working at breakneck speed, Dr. O, as he is known, has dermatology, if you'll excuse the pun, down to a science. A typical half-hour will see him treat a teen-ager for acne, administer facial silicone injections to a thirty-five-year-old New York model, complete a bald man's hair transplant, treat three dandruff cases and one psoriasis condition and complete a face-peeling and a dermabrasion.

Prices are high, but so is Dr. O's reputation, and his waiting room has seen the faces of New York's business giants, socialites and politicos—many of them there simply for a little help with their wrinkles. Treatment by nurses starts at twenty dollars plus medication, which Dr. O naturally sells from his own dispensary, so if you're up on your multiplication tables you'll get the message.

ART LINKLETTER

By the time Art Linkletter was twenty-nine, in the early 1940s, he was making one thousand dollars a week, but he wasn't happy, says *Forbes* in its July 15, 1969, issue. According to *Forbes*, he wanted the assurance of knowing that he'd always have money. Unlike most new-rich entertainers, he bought no sexy cars or flashy clothes; instead, he taught himself how to invest. His investing is done through Linkletter Enterprises, a professionally managed money firm which invests the funds of such TV personalities as Art Linkletter, Bob Cummings, Pat Boone and Cliff Robertson. Supposedly, they have $15 million—half invested in the stock market and the other half in deals.

Linkletter started in 1958 with, of all things, the Hula-Hoop. That was a good one, and, since then, he has been in everything from Royal Crown Cola to Bill Lear's steam car. He understands that big money is being made today out of change and betting on the right man. Linkletter told *Forbes* in 1969, "I like to take three or four guys like Bill Lear and bet on them. The thrill of one hit out of ten makes all of the other disappointments not only worth it emotionally, but one in ten makes back all the money I lost from the other nine, plus another ten times my initial investments."

What about his mistakes? He told *Forbes*, "Where I have missed most consistently and lost the most money all through my life was betting on a great salesman. You probably know the reason for that. A salesman, which I am, is more easily sold on dreams of another salesman." Good insight from a different kind of wheeler-dealer.

So You, Too, Want to Be a Wheeler-Dealer?

DAVID FROST

David Frost is another media man who became—or maybe always was, at heart—a wheeler-dealer. Arriving on the crest of the satire wave in Britain in the mid-1960s, Frost soon established himself on both sides of the Atlantic as a first-rate investigative TV journalist, while using the contacts he made in television to set up his own production companies, like Paradine Productions, which handled other artists and packaged TV shows.

A few years ago, he bought control of Hemdale, the entertainment company founded by actor David Hemmings and associates in the 1960s which produces movies, handles artists and even promotes fights. Still in his mid-thirties, Frost is a very rich man, and though he still appears on British television from time to time, the old sharpness, and therefore pulling power, has waned considerably. Perhaps these days he is more a businessman than a journalist, and his approach therefore is no longer radical but conservative.

Money as Motivation

What do all these very different personalities have in common and what is it that makes them wheeler-dealers? The answer is their motivations—money, ego gratification, social recognition and desire to have some fun out of life.

Ask a young businessman on the way up what is the key

Money, Ego, Power

motivation in his career, and in nineteen cases out of twenty, the answer will be the same—money. Money for possessions, money for a better life style, money for freedom, money to make more money.

And it is not difficult to see why money is the goal of so many young executives. From early on in your business life, you will probably feel victimized. You are a victim of circumstances, or of an unappreciative boss's whims, or even of the system, and the one thing that seems to separate you from the victimizers is money. With it, you have the freedom to be your own person, to move about as you wish, to say "screw it all" when the going gets tough. Without it, you are tied, choices are made for you and you are driven on by the basic needs to eat, sleep and care for your family.

From early on in your business life, too, you will see how prestige and position—both by-products of money, incidentally—entitle the bearer to a variety of extremely attractive fringe benefits: not merely a key to the senior executive washroom, but extravagant expense account meals, first-class travel and deluxe accommodation, chauffeur-driven limousines, all of which seem designed to lessen the pressures on a high-powered businessman. Obviously, these amenities appeal to any young man with an ounce of ambition and observing them firsthand inspires you to try and achieve them for yourself.

Temptation is still the original sin in the business world—though the bait is much more fattening than any apple—followed closely, and inevitably, by covetousness. Take, for example, your first business lunch as a young executive. The setting will probably be one of the

So You, Too, Want to Be a Wheeler-Dealer?

prestigious metropolitan lunch clubs or gourmet restaurants, where you will begin with exquisitely dry martinis and then proceed through several courses of superb rich food and excellent wine, and finish with brandy and choice cigars, totaling at least thirty dollars per person. If you have eaten all week at the local delicatessen for three dollars a day, it is not unreasonable that you aspire to eat such a luncheon every day—like your superiors—and, of course, at the expense of the company.

Or perhaps you are invited to a dinner party at your employer's home. The purpose of the meal might be to soften an angry client, but, for you, the evening provides the ultimate in orgiastic temptation. The pervading atmosphere is one of wealth and opulence in a setting of high-priced furnishings, exquisitely prepared food and impeccably dressed guests. Your senses sharpened by the experience, you will absorb your surroundings while vowing to yourself that one day you, too, will entertain as lord of the manor and partake of the good life.

Honest appraisal tells you that you are every bit as bright and talented as your superiors; so why should the difference of age or tenure prevent you from sharing the rewards that they enjoy?

From the outside looking in, or from the windowless corridor offices looking toward the executive penthouse suites, the transition from employee to employer looks easy enough to accomplish, and the benefits of success are more than enough of an incentive to make the climb.

Doodling on paper, you figure your yearly income minus mortgage payments, insurance and car payments. Crossing out the figures with resolve, you begin plotting your new net worth in terms of the $100,000-to-$150,000-a-year salary you imagine you'll soon be earning. The added money will allow for all kinds of necessary and exciting expenditures: some much-needed home improvements, or perhaps a newer and bigger house; certainly a new car, perhaps even a sports car; and that long-postponed vacation for maybe three weeks rather than two. And, finally, enough money to really make a substantial investment, to take a stand in a company, in order to earn some equity in the future.

On paper it looks easy. And in reality it seems within reach. All you really need is money. And judging from how quickly and easily others have made it, you *know* that you can do it, too, only faster, smarter and bigger than anyone else has ever done it before.

Gratifying Your Ego

Every man has a variety of needs which require satisfying in both the personal and the professional areas of his life. Perhaps the most complicated need—and certainly the most difficult to satisfy—is his ego.

Each of us has an image of himself and a certain amount of pride in the image we like to think that we project. It is when other people fail to respond to our images that we retaliate with a show of ego. Bragging and boasting is the easiest and quickest way of asserting your ego, but ultimately it offers only limited satisfaction as it is a very one-sided display. Becoming a wheeler-dealer provides the supreme ego trip—you see your own image

So You, Too, Want to Be a Wheeler-Dealer?

reflected back at you a hundred times a day by your surroundings, your life style, the effect you have on other people's lives, even by what they say about you—but of course it's a much more complex route to self-gratification.

The game begins with your everyday activities; meeting other businessmen, looking at new companies, studying financial statements, negotiating deals, planning mergers and acquisitions, disposing of unprofitable divisions, taking the helm of a company and steering it on an uncharted course. This is the kind of action that fuels an unquenchable ego.

At first, business associates, bankers, brokers and friends take notice of your activities and accord them praise, admiration or, more often than not, jealous glances. Later on in the game, as your activities take on greater proportions, magazines and newspapers, radio and television begin to notice and report news of your actions. Each new feat is accorded columns of print with full illustrations depicting you at various moments in your life. Your every other word is quoted—or, more likely, misquoted; your mother is asked to comment on your success, while she'd prefer to say a few words about how you hardly ever call her; and your every employee is eager to insert his two cents' worth. Just about the time that this national attention is going to your head and reaffirming your old opinion of your own greatness, your spouse will stop speaking to you.

Your mate resents your fame and recognition. After all, he or she (though with due regard for women's lib and women like Marion S. Kellogg, vice-president of

General Electric, most wheeler-dealers are male) knows you for what you really are: the one who falls asleep on the sofa attired in boxer shorts immediately following dinner, or the fellow who burps during meals and uses the wrong fork and water glass, or the man who can run a company of one thousand employees while the disciplining of a couple of children is beyond him. No man, as Anne Bigot de Cornuel wrote over three hundred years ago, is a hero to his valet—or, these days, to his wife.

Being the firsthand witness to your intimate failures and shortcomings, she has her own editorial opinion of your rave reviews. Jealousy reigns and the smug, self-righteous little woman sits back waiting eagerly for the first public scolding, the first knife in the back, the ridicule and condemnation, the knock-down that always follow on the heels of the star buildup in the press. And when it comes, be prepared to get it from both barrels on the home front.

"I told you so," and "I knew it all along," will be the first remarks greeting you at the door. Later, over dinner, between fistfuls of Gelusil, you'll be treated to such thought-provoking questions as, "What makes you think you're so great?" and "Why can't you be like all the other men at the country club?"

There you are, wheeling and dealing your way to ego gratification and success in the business world, while your greatest critic is deflating and defiling you within the walls of the $200,000 home she insisted you buy for her. Contentment with her share of the spoils from your

So You, Too, Want to Be a Wheeler-Dealer?

personal war on success is not enough. The egg-sized diamond solitaire, sable coats, designer clothing, expensive car and deluxe vacation are quickly devoured—but they leave an unmistakable aftertaste on the palate. She learns to live with, and love, the trappings of success, but the fact that only you can provide them for her is too bitter a pill for her to swallow.

She might deny her need for expensive goodies and tell you that she yearns for the simplicity of the life you shared before you became a mogul, but don't you believe it. What she really means is that she loves having you earn the money to pay the expenses but she prefers you to do it inconspicuously, quietly and not quite so brilliantly. And, oh yes, if you could find a way of mentioning that she had a hand in making you a success, it would make her feel ever so much better.

Your ego trip has triggered off *her* ego, leaving her feeling as incompetent, incomplete and untalented as she probably really is. She's insecure, and your seeming security amidst the fanfare and hullabaloo threatens her existence as she defines it.

Much of this will prove untrue, of course, if you are fortunate enough to have selected a mate who is intelligent and independent, a woman who is capable of handling her share of the home and family while pursuing her own interests and activities. But if yours is the woman who cannot get through a single day without a minor personal crisis, then you had better steel yourself against her inevitable attack.

MONEY, EGO, POWER

The Gentle Art of Social Climbing

There are people in the deal business for whom social recognition is probably the most important motivation. They are not content merely with enjoying a happy, healthy life and earning more than enough to provide everything they could possibly need or want. For them, being socially recognized, being part of the jet set, being numbered among the locomotives of society—"The Beautiful People" as Marylin Bender labeled them—is their ultimate goal.

It's having memberships to the most exclusive clubs, clothing by *the* couturier of the moment, invitations to the chicest parties, exquisite homes at the fashionable end of the fashionable streets in the most fashionable districts, photographs appearing on the society pages of the newspapers and magazines "seen enjoying a joke..." and, the ultimate, being on sufficiently intimate terms with a prince or duke or marquis to call him or her by their Christian name, that makes these people truly happy.

Money, of course, is the first prerequisite for membership of this group because money can buy anything—even friends and social position. If you were unlucky enough not to have been born into society, nor to have achieved that sort of standing through marriage, then all you can hope is that it will be thrust upon you in exchange for large sums of money spent in the right quarters.

But simply having money is by no means enough. You must have a certain amount of polish, savoir faire and

So You, Too, Want to Be a Wheeler-Dealer?

taste in order to make the grade and then maintain a position. It may be that you will need professional help —the services of someone *au fait* with the highest high society, like Earl Blackwell, society's public relations darling, or, at one time, that charming Russian, Colonel Serge Obolensky, whose influence ensures your being invited to the right parties and your being asked to serve on the right committees.

In addition, they can impose upon some of their other associates to see to it that when you begin throwing your little dinner parties only the *crème de la crème* of society will attend. Simultaneously, press releases and personal notes are sent to the columnists, supplying details of the evening.

Being recognized, belonging, being in, being where the action is, being totally *au courant*, being a luminary, is the essence of their game. And they play at it harder than they play backgammon at the Paradise Beach tournament or croquet on the sprawling Palm Beach lawns or golf in Palm Springs or dance at Jimmy'z in Monte Carlo. The sports are part of the game, too, and if you're proficient at any of them, it just might help you to get your foot in the door of one of the more exclusive clubs to which a membership is all important.

For the social climbing wheeler-dealers, being accepted by the *haut monde* is the moment of truth. It indicates they've made it. And by making it they have risen above their peers to a level of prestige and superiority. Part of the so-called *haut monde*, their egos are fed by their admiration of themselves as newly arrived socialites as well as by the esteem in which they imagine they are held by their former peers. High society becomes their playground. And their money is only important insofar as it purchases the wherewithal that permits them to play in style.

It's an ego trip, certainly, and eventually their social self-consciousness will lead them to think in terms of self-perpetuation. Contributing to society something of significance—be it a scholarship fund, an urban renewal project, a children's playground, a cultural foundation or a hospital wing—will perpetuate their name, gain them additional publicity and earn them a reputation for philanthropy, and, of course, it is all tax-deductible. It might be their ego trip, but at the same time groups of people who need help are benefiting from their donations. In a sense, the social climbers are repaying their debt to society—a debt incurred by having been offered admission.

Having Fun—and Getting Paid for It

Apart from the very real possibility of making a lot of money, wheeling and dealing can be great fun.

If you were offered the choice between holding down a five-day-a-week nine-till-five job in an insurance office or a bank, with little or no opportunity for travel or financial growth, and taking a job as director of mergers and acquisitions for a rapidly growing corporation seeking to expand its interests in other areas, maybe even other countries, working all hours and traveling constantly—which would you select? If it's the former, there's no point in reading any further!

So You, Too, Want to Be a Wheeler-Dealer?

Wheeling and dealing, getting involved in the tumult of corporate management, offers many more opportunities for the right kind of person to find his fulfillment, both professionally and personally. To succeed in business, and indeed in life, you must have a sense of humor, not only to help you through the tough times, but to keep you sane, and if you positively *enjoy* your work, that's a bonus that cannot be measured in terms of stock purchase plans or good retirement insurance. After all, people play Monopoly for fun in their spare time so you can imagine what it would be like to be playing it during office hours—and for real.

The true wheeler-dealer derives as much pleasure and satisfaction from the game—the deal business—as he does from "the prize," getting rich. Wheeling and dealing is not simply a means to an end, and only by throwing yourself wholeheartedly into your work will you get the satisfaction, the fun and the rewards that are there for the taking.

Understanding Your Motivations

It is easy to misunderstand the wheeler-dealer, and often hard to distinguish him from other businessmen or from promoters in general. Often, most of this confusion stems from not understanding the motivations of these men who have fought their way relentlessly to the top and, once on the pinnacle, have repeatedly risked both their fortunes and their futures by further attempts at scaling a new precipice. For some, it's money only, for

Money, Ego, Power

others it's power and money, and, for most, it's certainly ego. Which is the most important one for you? Money, ego, power—or is it all three? Make sure you understand yourself before you move forward because an understanding of what you want for yourself is absolutely essential to your success. Why fight your way to the top unless you know why you want to get there?

Let's look at a man who knew what he wanted. It wasn't money, but the power to be creative in an industry and in a company where he could have made a substantial contribution.

Phil Levin was a sixty-two-year-old wheeler-dealer when he made an attempt to take over Metro-Goldwyn-Mayer, now the property of Kirk Kerkorian. Levin, who made his fortune of around $75 million long before he was known to the business trade in New York and certainly before he became a wheeler-dealer, wanted to run a motion picture company. He decided on a proxy fight because he wanted the power to make changes. He had his own ideas as to what was wrong with MGM and the motion picture industry in general. Although he lost the proxy fight, he was obviously right about the motion picture industry and especially about MGM. He was right about the troubles in the industry long before anyone—even the long-time motion picture moguls—had realized what they were. And, in addition to his own personal gain of some $12 million profit on the sale of his MGM stock to the Bronfman/Time, Inc., interests, it is interesting to speculate on where MGM would have gone under Phil Levin's leadership instead of the Bronfman/Time, Inc., team. Maybe it would still be producing great

So You, Too, Want to Be a Wheeler-Dealer?

motion pictures; maybe Judy Garland's red shoes would still be in wardrobe.

It is important to understand that while it is true that Levin won in the traditional sense—that is, he made money from the deal—he lost in a personal way. He lost because what he really wanted was not to make more millions from the attack at MGM but to gain the power to use the ideas he had to change a company in the motion picture industry. For many wheeler-dealers, as for Levin in the MGM affair, profit is obviously in the back of their minds, but they are after more. Power. Power to be wielded toward a specific aim.

Phil Levin's motivation was specific. He wanted to make changes, and he was sure that they were the right ones. He lost out, but what is most important in all this is not so much that you win—but that you try, and that you can try under our system.

3

Preparing Yourself to Be a Wheeler-Dealer

Education

All the studies done so far on the relationship between earnings and education have indicated that there is a very direct correlation between the two—the higher the education, the higher the earnings. But, of course, it's not simply quantity that counts—it's quality and kind. If you plan to go into business, it makes sense to take courses in business studies, but additional courses in law or accounting will pay dividends and put you one step ahead of graduates in only one discipline. There is no one ideal course of education that will fit you for wheeling and dealing. Some outstandingly successful industrialists, like the late J. Paul Getty, favor the kind of Renaissance education that produces the well-rounded man, but others still insist on a suitable college degree followed by professional training in law or accounting.

Preparing Yourself to Be a Wheeler-Dealer

Certainly, most people in the deal business recommend training in one or the other, and each has its advocates. Many people argue that legal training is ideal since it instills a logical, rational approach to any problem and the necessary approach of looking at it from all angles. It also means that you know in advance what you can and cannot do in any deal (from a legal point of view), and this will not only save you a lot of money in outside legal fees but could prevent costly mistakes, and even lawsuits. Take the fabled Pritzker family; four generations of them have had legal training. As Jay Pritzker said, "We move quickly and assess risks without waiting for someone else to advise us. Lawyers can give you such useless advice. If you're not a lawyer, you're afraid there's something you ought to know."

And, of course, if you handle deals for other people in your capacity as attorney, you're in the best possible position to learn about the deal business from watching them in operation. There is no question that my best education came from first being the lawyer to the client rather than being the client myself. In my early years of law practice, I worked on almost every kind of deal—acquisition, sell-out, liquidation, merger and going public—in order to learn what it was all about. Some of my early work in proxy fights, which are no longer fashionable, gave me great insight into how a corporation really worked instead of the way it was supposed to work. Knowing what I could, or could not do, was a great advantage to me.

But there are drawbacks, like the natural pessimism that results from having defended so many actions that resulted from deals that went awry, and you instinctively approach any deal in terms of what might go wrong, rather than what might go right. Those who know a lot of lawyers know that "No, it can't be done" is the easy way out for the lawyer without risking the client; you can't get in trouble if you don't do it. Some lawyers just can't make the transaction; others may do it freely.

If you opt for training in accounting, as Jim Slater did, you will be able to glance at a balance sheet for a few moments and know at once whether the deal in question should be hotly pursued or quickly forgotten. And, with a financial background, assuming you also have flair, ambition and a keen business sense, you'll soon be able to learn quickly how to turn debits into credits, payables into receivables, and liabilities into assets.

And, of course, it isn't merely what you've learned that counts, but where you've learned it. If you believe that, in this egalitarian society of ours, a Juris Doctor from Brooklyn Law School carries the same cachet as a JD from Yale or Harvard, or even Oxford or Cambridge (remember how important it was to Gatsby's business contacts that he was an "Oggsford" man?), then just try peddling your Brooklyn degree within the hallowed portals of Mudge, Rose or Winthrop, Stimson, Putnam & Roberts, and see how long your preliminary interview lasts. No doubt about it, being an Ivy League man—or at least a graduate from one of the old, more distinguished institutions—still opens doors, and no serious would-be wheeler-dealer should think twice about exploiting every ounce of prestige and one-upmanship that such a degree carries.

Preparing Yourself to Be a Wheeler-Dealer

Don't think, though, that your education is completed when you graduate from college. Learn from everybody with whom you come into contact because there is no substitute for experience—yours or other people's. Study the empire builders of the past, the Rockefellers, the Vanderbilts, the Fords, and see how they made their millions. True, that was in the heady days before 1934 and the introduction of new kinds of rules and regulations to protect investors, when business was a free-for-all, but great fortunes have been made since 1934, and the wheeler-dealers of the 1960s and 1970s were the men who learned to operate within the framework of those rules and, where necessary, to bend them a little. Strategies may change, but the general *modus operandi* remains the same. As Charles Luckman said back in 1958: "Success is still the old ABC—ability, breaks and courage."

Moving in the Right Circles

Most people divide their lives into two distinct areas—business and pleasure—but for the truly ambitious young man, the distinction is an artificial one. "It's not what you know, it's who you know" is an old cliché but, like so many old clichés, it's achieved that status because it's true. Meeting the right people—people in a position to influence your career in the long term as well as the short—is not only valuable, but it is also essential if you want to make your first million by the time you reach your early thirties and haven't the time to progress through the usual channels. Through leisure and social pursuits you can meet people whom you'd find it almost impossible to get to know on a strictly professional basis.

Like your career, your social life needs to be thought about and worked at. You might enjoy spending your free time with old friends from the Bronx or from Rochester, but you won't be using it constructively. That doesn't mean you must drop your old friends completely. Nobody likes a snob, and besides, even they might prove useful to you in your career one day. Map out a social career for yourself that matches your business career in terms of ambition.

Since it is extremely unlikely that the right people will seek you out, you must infiltrate their ranks. One of the easiest ways of doing that is to involve yourself in a project they support, whether it's charity, politics or the arts. Not only will it give you the opportunity to meet them on an informal basis and give you common ground, it will also give you an opportunity to demonstrate your creativity, initiative and capacity for hard work to prospective clients or employers, even though they don't yet realize that's what they are.

One demonstration is worth a dozen protestations at a personnel interview, and if you feel that your manner or appearance might block your future advancement, it may be the only way of overcoming that particular obstacle. One young man whose brash manners would probably have terminated his personnel interview in five minutes under other circumstances got the job he was after because one of the company's executives had worked with him on a charity fund-raising committee and had

Preparing Yourself to Be a Wheeler-Dealer

been impressed with his proven ability. If you do get involved in voluntary work for this reason, then don't sell the committee short. Always try to be constructive in your approach, and when the opportunity arises, put forward your ideas with tact and assurance. The way you present your case at a committee meeting will give any prospective employer a clear indication of the way you work.

Be sure, too, that you are 100 percent reliable. If you're not prepared to work hard and do what you promise to do, then you'd be better off not getting involved in the first place. It's just as easy to create a negative impression as it is to create a positive one.

Making Friends and Building Your Team

Now that you're moving in the right circles, you must decide which are the friends to be made, the people to be influenced. What should dictate your choice is no longer how much you like someone personally but how useful they might be to you in your career. That may sound calculating, if not downright ruthless, but it's human nature to use other people to a greater or lesser extent. And while it doesn't actually justify it, it's worth remembering that other people are almost certainly using you.

So, with a clear conscience, begin to cultivate the people most likely to be of use to you. That executive from the Chase Manhattan may not be the world's greatest conversationalist but a more-than-passing acquaintance with him cannot help but improve your chances of getting a loan. If he himself isn't in a position to help directly, his recommendation to a colleague who is may well be the deciding factor in your getting that loan. Think ahead, and don't concentrate on the short term. You may find one man easy to get on with and very useful to you at this point in your career, but don't ignore the man he's with, who may be older and much more difficult to get to know. For one thing, you may find you need him in five or ten years' time and, for another, you could learn a lot from his experience by talking to him now.

But you shouldn't only be seeking out people who are in a position to use their influence on your behalf. You should be looking for people to work with you, to be part of your future team. And you *will* need a team: people working in groups are more effective than people working alone because what one misses, the other will pick up, and when one approach to a problem fails, another might succeed. You must learn to delegate authority efficiently and divide the different functions of management among those best suited to handle them. No one is an expert in every field, no matter how talented he may be. "If you have a problem," said Leonard Lauder, president of Estée Lauder, "find someone better than you to solve it. There are people here who are better at twenty different things than I. The best education for me was the knowledge that you can always get someone better than you to solve it."

Although you are some way from your first deal, it isn't too early to start assembling a team around you. Seeing how a man copes with a small problem is a good indica-

Preparing Yourself to Be a Wheeler-Dealer

tion of how he'll cope with a larger one, and better to weed out your associates now while you're still small-time than wait till you're already into your first deal and then discover that there is a weak link in your chain. Basically, you'll need an attorney (you can dispense with him if you are one), an accountant, a certified one is best, a stockbroker or merchant banker, and experts on insurance, taxes and various kinds of banking.

Early in your career, the company you work for will probably have dealings with firms that specialize in those areas. Watch out for the bright young men who stand out from the crowd, those who seem more eager to work than the rest, who have sharp, inquisitive minds. If possible, try to get them assigned to work in your own particular area so that you can see at first hand how they operate and assess their potential value to you later on.

If you haven't had any contact through your company with the top professional firms, then hire one of the most prestigious to handle your problems. If it's an accounting problem, then try a firm like Touche Ross or Clarence Rainess & Company. Since you'll be a comparatively small client, they'll probably assign some of their more junior accountants to look after you—young men, like you, just starting out on their careers, with plenty of ambition, exactly the kind of people you'll eventually want on your team.

Selecting an attorney or an accountant isn't simply a question of finding someone competent to do the job. More important is to find someone with objectivity, who won't let his self-interest influence the advice he gives you. It's virtually impossible to understand what motivates any individual to reach a particular decision but, unless you're prepared to go to the lengths of hiring an outside testing organization to carry out motivational tests, all you can do is ask yourself: "Why should he recommend this course of action? What's in it for him?" If you cannot see any obvious self-interest at work, then chances are his advice is objective.

Once you've assembled your team of legal and financial advisers, it's up to you to exploit them properly, to make use of their knowledge and experience and not let them make use of yours. You must lay down the guidelines within which they work, and you must initiate policy—don't wait for them to offer suggestions. If you've chosen your team wisely, you'll be surrounded by talented, ambitious people, and if you're not careful you'll find that your lawyer or accountant is the one who is wheeling and dealing and well on his way to his first million while you still haven't managed to get off the ground.

When Jim Slater was getting going in 1960, he realized the necessity for what he called a "proper organization." Slater's approach was "to organize, delegate and supervise," and by early 1969 he had built a small office team of nearly two hundred people who were responsible for the main operational activities of his company. Jim Slater regarded himself as the leader of a young and successful group of entrepreneurs and he considered the success of the company the result of good team work.

Commenting on his approach he said:

Preparing Yourself to Be a Wheeler-Dealer

The people one employs in an executive capacity divide broadly into idea men and functionaries. The idea men are the most difficult to motivate and retain. Usually they are very able and creative people, who basically want to "do their own thing." They are motivated in the first instance by being able to develop their talents within the organization in a relatively free way. We always give them a lot more responsibility than they would find elsewhere. They are also motivated financially with share option schemes and, in certain instances, shares in specific projects in which they are involved. Certain people do, of course, develop an absolute compulsion to "do their own thing" in their own way outside our organization. I have found that the best way of dealing with this is always to have an open door, and be willing to back them in their new ventures as opposed to trying to stop them from branching out. As far as the functionaries are concerned, they are, of course, vitally important to the success of the organization, but they are usually very much more easy to motivate and retain.

Slater's concern for the people who worked for him and his ability to recognize their needs and accomplishments often inspired the employees to produce beyond their already fine capacities. In addition, this approach earned him their loyalty and respect. When Slater tendered his resignation, the team he had worked so hard to build was sorry to see him go.

MONEY, EGO, POWER

Selecting the Right Job to Get Started

Selecting the right job is almost as important as selecting the right mate. The consequences of that choice are certainly as far-reaching and the choice should be undertaken with just as much care. A wrong decision at this stage could mean several wasted years simply coasting along in a dead-end situation. When you're job-hunting, you should explore four main situations:

LEARN AT THE HAND OF A MASTER

There is no substitute for good, old-fashioned experience, and the best way to obtain it is by working for one of the all-time great entrepreneurs. Not only will the first-hand experience you gain by watching a master in action be invaluable, you can also learn a great deal from the wealth of *his* past experience. So many of this generation of wheeler-dealers have learned their craft from ITT President Harold Geneen—among them, David Mahoney of Norton Simon, George Strickman of Colt Industries, John C. Loeb of Crucible Steel—that they're often referred to as the alumni of Geneen University. Working for a man like Larry Tisch at Loew's would offer you an education in the running of hotels and movie theaters, real estate companies, banks and insurance, while a couple of years with Charles Bluhdorn at Gulf + Western would teach you how to succeed in the movie business, and everything else, by trying very hard, and, with luck, how to avoid losing those profits in the record business. You'd also learn that while cosmetics are glamorous, it's the zinc mines and the auto parts that make the money.

FINDING A COMPANY IN TROUBLE

If you're talented, ambitious and can assess whether the company is salvageable—or indeed worth salvaging—this could be a real shortcut to success. By maneuvering yourself into a position near the top, you're perfectly placed not only to observe, and learn from, a corporation's life-and-death struggle but, also, to move into the top job if the present incumbent is fired or quits before the situation kills him. Obviously, a situation like this is fraught with danger, but if, as well as talent and ambition, you also have nerves of steel and an iron digestion, it's worth a try. Had you worked for Mac Clifford at Curtis Publishing back in 1968, you might have been the man to save the company, pay off the bank debt and go down in history as the man who killed *The Saturday Evening Post*.

HELP THE OLD MAN RETIRE

A company whose president is close to retiring age (especially if he has no sons or daughters hovering in the wings ready to take over) is also worth careful consideration. Don't wait too long, though. Make your move in plenty of time to learn everything you can from the aging president and to have given him at least half a dozen good reasons to put your name forward when the subject of choosing his successor comes up. But don't devote all your energies to cultivating him. The other members of the board are the ones who'll have to vote you in, and, if you want to run the company successfully, you'll need the support of the other executives too.

Do make sure that the old man really is about to retire before you make your move. The fact that he's old doesn't necessarily mean he's about to abdicate. Look at all those who waited for Charles Revson of Revlon to retire and who never made it. Not only had he shown no intention of retiring, but he also neglected to develop what his critics call any "depth of management," and then, when he was fatally ill, he brought in a man from the outside who had ITT experience. Obviously, he believed that no one on the inside was capable of succeeding him.

RUN WITH A FAST-MOVING COMPANY

Anyone who had the insight to realize the potential of Xerox or Polaroid fifteen years ago, and to jump on those bandwagons, couldn't help but succeed brilliantly. If another such opportunity presents itself, and the analysis of its potential for growth in terms of future service possibilities is good, then seize it with both hands. Be wary of staying too long; get out while the company is still booming and don't wait till a hot idea begins to cool down. As Bernard Baruch advised, "Sell while the stock

Preparing Yourself to Be a Wheeler-Dealer

is still going up." Take your profits and buy into, or start up, another fast-moving company.

Acquiring a Reputation

By now, if you have applied what you've learned, you should have begun to acquire some kind of reputation, hopefully a positive one. After all, your reputation is all you have to offer in exchange for employment, or backing—both moral and financial—and if it's negative, it's highly unlikely that you'll get any further.

No matter how limited your experience in business may be, your work will have created an impression on your immediate superior, if on no one else. Ideally, if he were writing you a job recommendation tomorrow, he should be able to say that you are bright, reliable, responsible, punctual, hard-working, loyal, honest, persevering, enterprising, creative, ambitious, aggressive, cooperative. In fact, if he had any sense, he'd tear up that job recommendation and try to persuade you to stay with a higher salary and a more responsible job. If you have proven yourself to be all those things, it's unlikely that the fact will have gone unnoticed by other executives in the company.

But it is no good simply *having* all those qualities; you must be seen to have them too—or, to put it another way, it's not simply what you do, it's the way that you do it. Suppose your boss has asked you to look over a report he's prepared for a board meeting that day. You do, and not only is it much too long, but he's forgotten one of the key points. You could hand it back to him just before the meeting and say, "It's boring and you've forgotten to mention the tax loss carry-forward," or you could go to him the first thing in the morning and say, "I think a lot of that detail will be wasted on the board, and, by the way, do you have that section on the tax loss carry-forward? It doesn't appear to be here." Behave in the first manner and you've made yourself an enemy. Behave in the second and, assuming that your boss is perceptive enough to realize what's happening (why else would you be working for him?), you'll not only have impressed him with your sharpness but with your loyalty, too.

Establishing Credit

Although you might think you are years away from your first deal, now is the time to set about establishing credit, and the only way to do it is by borrowing money from a bank and, of course, paying it back. The more you borrow (and pay back), the higher your credit rating will be.

Naturally, the kind of bank from which you attempt to borrow is important, and, for preference, choose a well-established bank, like the Morgan Guaranty and Trust Company. That was the first lesson I taught my wife, before we were married, in her postgraduate course in wheeling and dealing, and her experiences at Morgan are worth recording:

> According to instructions, I went off to Morgan and inquired about opening an account. I was intro-

Preparing Yourself to Be a Wheeler-Dealer

duced to an amiable vice-president whose smile faded rapidly when I told him that I wished to transfer my checking and savings accounts to his bank.

Although he tried to lure my money across the street to the New York Bank for Savings, where, he informed me, I could acquire a gift of an electric blanket with my new account, I held my ground. "This is a lovely bank, very tastefully decorated, and I work in the building," I pointed out. "Besides, the lines at Chemical are getting much too long and this place is always relatively empty."

Seeing that I could not be swayed, he began fumbling for the necessary forms. "You realize, madam, that you must open an account with a minimum balance of three thousand dollars, and the account may never go below that sum." I didn't know that, but I told him, "That's no problem."

Not one to give in gracefully, he hissed, "We only pay four and a half percent interest; the bank across the street pays five percent, and they give you a passbook while we only send a monthly statement." "I'm always afraid of losing my passbook, anyway," I said with a sweet smile.

And so I became a patron of Morgan—much to the chagrin of the amiable vice-president—and my credit rating soared. Next time I purchased a block of stock with a new broker and reported my bank reference, he assured me grandly, "Oh, Morgan, that's just fine."

I had established what Mr. Ackerman called "instant credit," and from then on in I was off and running. In fact, only recently when I withdrew my wheeling-and-dealing-fattened accounts from Morgan to move to a more convenient bank, the amiable vice-president informed me that they "were indeed very sorry to see me leave their bank."

It may seem rather pointless to go through all that hassle when you don't actually need to borrow money yet, but the reason for doing so is simple; you are establishing credit in preparation for the day when you will need a substantial loan to finance your first deal. Since you have the money, and are paying for the privilege in interest charges, you might just as well put it to good use, not only to pay for itself but to make you a profit, as well. It's called leverage—the art of using other people's money to make money for yourself—and it works like this. If you borrow $100 from a bank at 7 1/2 percent interest and invest it at a return of 15 percent, at the end of a year you'll have $15, of which you owe the bank $7.50, leaving you with a profit of $7.50 for your efforts. Obviously, if you can do it with $50,000 or $100,000, you see what profit is all about. Today, you can buy good bonds yielding 8 1/2 percent to 10 percent, and borrow from banks at 7 percent or less.

Basically, the principle is: Never buy anything for cash —whether it's a new car, a house or a company—if you can borrow the money and use the cash that you have to earn enough to pay for the loan and make you a profit.

a) If I took a $40,000 mortgage on my house at 7 1/2 percent and invested the $40,000 in high-grade bonds at 10 percent, over the life of the mortgage's twenty-five years I could earn $1000 a year for twenty-five years, or $25,000.

b) If I took the $40,000 and put it into a good dollar fund which has traditionally earned an average of 9 percent, I would earn $600 a year for twenty-five years, or $15,000.

c) If I took the $40,000 and put it into my first deal, maybe I would earn 1000 percent!

Take the example of a woman who owns a cooperative apartment in Paris, bought a few years ago for $200,000. Today, that apartment is worth at least $400,000. Her question was, "Should I sell my apartment because I never seem to have enough money to live on?" Well, the exercise is always the same. If she were to sell the apartment and put her money into safe Eurodollar bonds, she would have 10 percent on $400,000 or $40,000 a year in cash income. But where would she live? Well, the answer to that question was that she could rent a very nice apartment for $20,000 a year, maybe not as grand, but nice enough. The arithmetic is quite simple: sell the apartment and have $20,000 extra to spend, or to put into your first deal.

If you're seriously interested in learning the art of borrowing money for fun and profit, then either talk to a good banker or read some of the many specialized books on the market. It isn't difficult to grasp, but too many factors are involved to be covered here. Basically, what you need to know is: who lends money—commer-

MONEY, EGO, POWER

cial banks, savings and loan companies, credit unions and finance companies; how they lend it—through personal, business or collateral loans, for instance; what they charge (interest) and on what basis they will lend the money to you. There is no question that without credit —or a rich family—it's hard to get started. But banks are in the business of lending money; you have to give them a good reason, though I think you will be surprised at how easy it is to borrow once you know how to do it. Remember, you are as good as your credit, which means as good as your record for paying back what you borrow.

There is still no question that getting that first stake is always the hardest part of any deal. Ask any banker and he will tell you that it's easier to borrow money if you already have money; the difficult part is getting that first sum of money. It's like going on your first job interview; no one will hire you if you haven't had previous experience, but how can you get any experience if no one will give you that first job?

Let me tell you about my own experience. When I was starting out in 1959, I gave a great deal of thought to this problem. It seemed to me that there were lots of ways to make money if only I could get some capital to help get me started. At that time, my office was in the Seagram Building at 375 Park Avenue in New York. If you know the area, you are aware that the building is within a hundred yards of at least ten different banks. One morning on my way to work, a sign in one of the bank windows caught my eye, and I decided that it was high time to find out if I could borrow some money.

By lunchtime, I had devised a master plan. My first

Preparing Yourself to Be a Wheeler-Dealer

stop was First National City Bank, now called Citibank, where I had a small personal checking account. In I went and instead of depositing or withdrawing my usual sums from my checking account, I went straight to the personal loan department located downstairs, where a young lady brought me to the desk of some obscure assistant assistant vice-president. I introduced myself as a young lawyer working across the street in the Seagram Building and announced that I wished to borrow some money.

The banker asked what the money was for and I told him that I was planning to make some repairs on my house, which was a real stretch of the truth since I didn't even own a house and was living then in a $130-a-month apartment in Riverdale. The banker seemed pleased with my response and when he asked how much I wanted to borrow, I asked what the maximum was. He gave me a figure of $10,000 on a personal loan, and we agreed that I would take the full $10,000 amount.

After filling out the forms, but being careful not to say anything about owning a house, and using some of the creative accounting that I had learned in law school, I soon had my $10,000 repayable over thirty-six months with an interest rate that has been blocked from my mind because it was so high.

With my $10,000 check from First National, I went back to the office and thought some more about my plan. The $10,000 was a good beginning but most of the moneymaking investments that I had in mind required at least ten times that amount to even get started. I went downstairs to the Brasserie, had a bowl of hearty onion soup and crusty French bread, summoned up my courage and walked out the revolving door of the restaurant through the revolving door of Manufacturers Hanover.

This time I headed for the "new accounts" department and, with check in hand, I climbed the stairs to the mezzanine, where a smart-looking assistant vice-president greeted me and my money. I introduced myself as an attorney working in the Seagram's Building and said I would like to open an account—a personal checking account—with the $10,000 check that I had with me. Within the space of two hours, I had become successively a creditor at First National City and a depositor at Manufacturers Hanover.

Somehow, although the money was not really mine, I felt sure that I was on to a good plan. This borrowing of money didn't seem so difficult after all, and now I was at least a man of substance at Manufacturers Hanover with a $10,000 checking account—a sum that seemed quite enormous to me as a young lawyer who was earning less than that for a full year's work.

The next day, lunchtime was a busy period once again. After a quick lunch of *croque monsieur* and coffee I was off again on my appointed rounds. This time it was a matter of borrowing money from Chemical Bank and depositing at the Bank of New York. The second day everything went smoothly; I knew the routine, had had my financial statement typed in the office and had ready answers to all the questions that I knew I'd be asked. The total after two days was $20,000 borrowed and $20,000 deposited. That was a Friday, and I decided to give my plan a rest over the weekend to figure out if I still thought it was

Preparing Yourself to Be a Wheeler-Dealer

sound. I spent a busy weekend with the pencil figuring out what the interest was costing me each day for the money borrowed, whether I could afford it and how much of my interest was deductible in terms of my particular tax bracket.

By Monday, I was back on the bank circuit. Fortified by a lunch of *pfannkuchen* and white wine at the Brasserie, I paid a visit to Bankers Trust to borrow another $10,000, which was then deposited in the neighboring Chase Manhattan. Then I decided to stop for a while, let the deposits and loans cool off and get my mind onto other things. I figured that with $30,000 borrowed, I was starting to get the kind of credit line that I deserved. At that time, the interest rate was probably around 6 1/2 percent, so I needed $1950 in interest on an annual basis, plus cash for the repayment schedule, to keep my plan operative.

After about ninety days, I started on Phase Two of my "plan for instant borrowing." I began a round of visits to all the banks where I now had my deposit accounts—Manufacturers Hanover, Bank of New York and Chase Manhattan. At each of these banks I had a short meeting with my "banker" and asked him about the possibility of obtaining a loan. The reply was a confident one: with your account, I am sure that we can lend you money . . . How much do you need? I never did say just how much I really wanted, but I decided that $10,000 from each one would be just fine. After signing the notes, the terms of which I now knew by heart, I started on my way back to the original three banks from which I had first borrowed $10,000 each. At each branch where I was then listed as a borrower—First National City, Chemical and Bankers Trust—I deposited, as conspicuously as possible, $10,000. Throughout the process at each bank, I tried to get to know one bank officer, who would remember me by name the next time that I came into the bank.

By now, my little black record book listed borrowings at $60,000 and deposits at $60,000. After about six months, I decided that it was about time to start repaying some of my personal loans, pulling down my deposits as needed. I would talk to my friendly assistant vice-president, tell him that things were great and that I was having a terrific year collecting a couple of really big fees on cases and that I would like to prepay my loan. Now, if you know bankers as well as I do after twenty years of borrowing money, you know that there is nothing that a banker likes better than having a loan repaid before it comes due. You see, every loan made represents a risk to the bank, and to prove to an examiner—be it an internal or external bank examiner—that a loan is good, it must be repaid by its due date. A prepayment represents just that many more "Brownie points" and makes the banker's judgment appear that much more secure. Understand the process of "take" and "pay"; it's the key to understanding how a bank works and how you go about establishing credit. It's not your net worth nor the collateral that really counts because banks are not in the business of foreclosing. What matters is your record and whether or not you, the borrower, keep your word.

At every bank in which you do business, you are judged by two criteria: how much are your average free balances (noninterest earning deposits) and how good is

Preparing Yourself to Be a Wheeler-Dealer

your payment record. This running financial record is kept over the years just in the way your doctor keeps your medical record, and if your record is a good one, then the bank's facilities open to meet your needs.

It's obviously a costly business to build a line of credit. Although after a while you can deposit your funds in interest-bearing accounts, at the beginning, it is your free balances that determines your value as a customer. Therefore, you have to pay out of income for the privilege of establishing a credit line. It's not really all that bad when you take into consideration that your omnipresent, omniscient U.S. tax collector allows you to deduct up to $10,000 of interest from your tax return under the new law. And with an earned income bracket of 35 to 50 percent, the government is paying a good portion of your costs in building your credit line.

Starting with this one $10,000 personal loan, I then moved from the personal loan department downstairs to the commercial loan department upstairs, where the interest rate is lower and the repayment terms less onerous. After about eighteen months, my credit line was about $100,000 at the six banks, and it was then that I decided to launch my investment plan. I was a good customer at each of the banks, I always repaid what I borrowed—often before the actual due date, and after a while I could clean up at each of the banks by using the borrowings from the other banks. In the beginning, I used only a portion of my borrowings for investments, keeping a good cash reserve on hand at all times to pay back any borrowings when needed.

I looked for short-term investments like the stock market or loans to friends or clients who seemed dependable. I understood the basic fact about investments, that the rewards were commensurate with the risks. And since I was playing with "other people's money" (OPM), I needed safe investments. Also, I knew that at all times my investment would have to be kept liquid because I needed cash at different times to pay back my short-term indebtedness. If you need cash to pay back a short-term bank loan, you cannot invest your money on a long-term basis. More people have gone broke making that mistake: borrowing "short" and investing "long."

At the same time, my salary was on the increase and I was being offered small pieces of big deals that were recommended to me by my clients. The cumulative effect was the increasing of my net worth by the use of the bank's capital. Quite quickly the word got around that I had some capital—not much by today's standards of operations—but you would be surprised how far $5000 can go when someone needs the money now and not a minute later. From the bank's point of view, my accounts showed lots of activity with frequent increasing balances —even if they only lasted a couple of weeks. At the end of a couple of years, I was in the position of knowing that my record at the banks justified a $100,000 line of credit on a practically unsecured basis.

I would never take too much from one bank—maybe a maximum of $25,000—because bankers have a very tough time with their superiors in justifying any unsecured credits. But when you combine your lines of credit from six banks or more, you suddenly find yourself with a lot of money available to invest.

Preparing Yourself to Be a Wheeler-Dealer

Using Paper Money

Paper money means, basically, the shares in your company. Provided a market can be established for your company's stock, then those shares can be used as money. But, you might well say, why would anyone take your shares instead of cash? That's where the essence of the deal business really begins. Your ability to sell yourself and your company's shares when you are making a deal, instead of parting with the company's valuable cash holdings, is the name of the game.

In a rising market, it is not difficult to persuade a seller to accept shares instead of cash since he can make an almost instant profit. In a falling market, it is impossible. A seller with any sense will insist on cash.

Understanding the effective use of paper money is the key to success or failure in wheeling and dealing. And to see the effective use of noncash at its most brilliant, just study the career of Meshulam Riklis of Rapid American.

An emigrant from Israel, he arrived in the United States in 1947 with only $4000 in his pocket. His first job, in Columbus, Ohio, was teaching Hebrew and mathematics, but his sights were always set on a different career. "I always wanted to go into business," he has said. "When I was a kid in Tel Aviv, they used to call me the Minister of Finance."

And at the first opportunity he got out of teaching and took a part-time job, first as a security analyst, then as a customers' man with Piper, Jaffray and Hopwood, a brokerage firm in Minneapolis. He used his contacts in the Jewish community to build his customer base. He has never hesitated to press his Jewishness, and he's proud of his Israeli background. Like all brokers, he soon discovered that his customers were willing to give him money if he could give them quick results in capital gains. He learned quickly, and understood that being a broker was just being the middleman; he made a commission, but the big profit always belonged to someone else. He started with the concept of undervalued companies and dreamed of a billion-dollar empire. It was easy in that era to pick the companies, but his extraordinary ability in selling himself is really what got him in. This worked both ways: in building close friends to supply needed capital, and then convincing the seller to sell at the right price and on the right terms.

His well-known theory, called "the effective nonuse of cash," is really standard repertoire for wheeler-dealers because they don't have any cash. Rik is frank when he says there are two kinds of money: hard cash and paper money. Early in the game, he explains, he established as a principle "not to pay cash for a company that cannot immediately generate at least a similar amount of cash for the next move. If, however, such an acquisition is desirable but cannot produce the cash, then it has to be acquired via another method of financing." Ideally, of course, says *Forbes* in 1971, Riklis never used cash at all; he used paper money wherever he could.

Preparing Yourself to Be a Wheeler-Dealer

Becoming Chairman of the Board or President

In preparing yourself to be a wheeler-dealer there are two positions within the company that should ultimately interest you—chairman of the board and president. These are the positions that wield the most power, and the men who hold them control the destiny of the company.

On paper, at least, every corporation is controlled by its board of directors. As corporation law now stands, every company must have a board, and the directors are usually elected by the stockholders, though there are exceptions. If a director also happens to be a stockholder and owns over 51 percent of the stock, the board can then control its own reelection.

Both the chairman of the board and the president of the corporation are elected by the board members, and either one could be appointed chief executive officer. In any number of companies the chairman, president and chief executive officer are the same person. In theory, most corporations operate on a consensus basis, but, in fact, it is the board of directors that makes the important decisions and passes them on to the company's executives for implementation.

As chief executive officer and chairman of the board you control the nominations for election to the board. And, if you have any sense at all, you will nominate those men over whom you have some influence and who are likely to support your decisions. Often, your employees, who depend on you for their livelihood, or certain stockholders or businessmen for whom your company represents a potentially lucrative source of business make the most loyal and supporting directors.

Of course, you won't find many company directors who will admit that this is the case in their company—nobody likes to admit that he is in the top man's pocket—but it happens in the best of companies. After all, what would be the point of nominating a board of directors who would oppose your every move?

In some cases, of course, the individual integrity of board members is unimpeachable. Take Eastman Kodak, for instance, where the general assumption is that the board would resign rather than acquiesce to any strong-arm tactics from the chief executive—but, in the final analysis, this is no real brake on the chief executive's power, as the case of Penn Central showed only too clearly. For years, its board had a stature and prestige almost unrivaled in the business world, yet it was powerless to oppose the wishes of the management, so that, ultimately, the only option left open to its members was resignation. There are numerous examples of boards of directors rendered powerless by one strong personality at the top, either by virtue of his large stockholding or his management genius or simply the forcefulness of his personality.

Take the case of Singer, which was dominated for almost twenty years by one man, Donald P. Kircher, wholly through his strong personality. The outside directors did nothing until Kircher was virtually carried home from the office, too weak to work. Only then, when the company had become a shambles, did they summon up enough courage to present the ailing chairman with an ultimatum—either resign or get fired. In the case of RCA, the showdown was a long time in coming, but there too the directors finally got around to firing the founder's son, Robert Sarnoff.

In practice, therefore, most companies are controlled not by their directors, but by one man or a small group of men who make the decisions and initiate policy; the function of the board is, more or less, to rubber-stamp them for the sake of appearances.

While the board may be powerless in practice to effect changes in management, stockholders, if they should become thoroughly disenchanted with the way their investment is being managed, are anything but that. If they decide to tender their stock to someone anxious to take control of the company, then the situation at the top will change very quickly and a new chairman and president, who have the confidence of the stockholders, will be elected.

Larry Tisch, surprisingly, is a great champion of Stockholder Power. If he had his way, no management would be safe from challenge by its stockholders, and incumbent executives would be forbidden to spend more than a nominal amount on defending themselves against proxy fights. "We've lost the concept that the stockholders own the company. If you want to change management, you're a raider and the next thing to a criminal is a raider!"

But having worked your way to the top, you want to stay there, and there are two ways of ensuring that you do. First, you or your family should own over 51 percent of the stock. Failing that, you should introduce a staggered voting system. Under this system, instead of the whole board of directors coming up for election each year, only a third, say, or a fifth of them do, so it will take three or five years for the whole board to change and for control of the company to pass into other hands. The main advantages of the system are that it discourages proxy fights and wards off those nasty "raiders" from the outside.

If one wanted to pick one wheeler-dealer out of the many who knows the advantages of the "corporate system" better than anyone else, one would have to pick Victor Posner. Posner, who dropped out of school when he was thirteen years old to work with his father, who owned five food stores in Baltimore, is the "Ivan the Terrible" of the corporate raiders. You may disagree with Larry Tisch, Meshulam Riklis or Charles Bluhdorn, but you hate Victor Posner. Often, when a major company finds out that Victor Posner is interested in it, it becomes almost psychotic.

Posner, the self-made man, has been successful as a wheeler-dealer for quite a few years: first, as a developer of single-family homes in Baltimore, later as a developer of row houses and then as a speculator in Florida real estate. In 1965, Posner took an interest in DWG, a Detroit cigar-maker, which began his career as corporate empire builder. From there, it has been up, all the way.

Victor Posner's business methods could be the subject of a lengthy book by itself, but one thing about Posner: he doesn't come cheap. Posner, who may pay himself as much as $700,000 a year in salary, has been accused by stockholders of his various companies of taking more

Preparing Yourself to Be a Wheeler-Dealer

than a million a year from all of his companies combined. Posner's answer to all of this criticism is to ignore it, with the assertion that he works from sunrise to sunset, never takes a vacation, lost his wife in a divorce and that, in fact, the companies he works for get a bargain when you measure his performance against the others who operate similar companies. In addition to his dividends, Posner takes a lot of extras, which he obviously believes go with the job. He moves from coast to coast in a private jet, and I am sure that almost all of his other expenses are picked up by one of his corporations. After all, if he works from sunrise to sunset, they all must be "business" expenses.

Although Victor Posner is a wealthy man, with his corporate setup he probably is as well off as a man who has five times his net worth.

If you think that Victor Posner is the only wheeler-dealer who lives off his corporation, as chairman or president, you are sadly mistaken. Most of the executives who work for corporations—or own them—not only receive salary, but also receive all sorts of bonuses, either in stock, cash or expenses. Whatever form these extras take, though, every chairman or president participates in them.

Milan Panic spent his formative years learning how to survive in his native Yugoslavia. But once he came to America in 1955, he was quick to understand the rules of wheeling and dealing. Starting with virtually nothing in 1956, he has moved, in twenty years, into the big time, and his company, International Chemical & Nuclear Corporation, hopes to do $500 million in sales this year.

In exchange for his talents and devotion to duty, as

chairman of the board, Panic expects the corporation to make his life as easy for him as it possibly can. Although he owns a forty-two-room baronial home just outside Pasadena, his second home is near Geneva, and rather than "commute" between homes and offices (in New York and Los Angeles, as well as Pasadena) in commercial airplanes, and thereby run the risk of losing precious working time in delays, the company provides him with a private Lockheed Jet Star, which, he says, he uses like a telephone. And you know how much telephone calls can cost today.

Though he, personally, runs a Rolls-Royce, a Cadillac and a BMW motor bike, the company lays on a fleet of Mercedes SL 600s to ferry him from his various local airports to his various offices and homes, which must add a considerable amount of spending power to the $300,000 salary the company also pays him.

Acquiring Equity

Another concept you must understand in preparing yourself is the nature of equity, or, to put it in layman's terms, a piece of the action.

Equity means the amount of stock you hold in your company. The more stock you own, the greater your equity. As chief executive officer, acquiring equity should be your major personal goal. A large paycheck, plus an unlimited expense account and all the other fringe benefits are all very well, but there is no substitute for owning a stake in the company. It is the difference between security and insecurity. It is what will enable you to retire while you are still young enough and fit enough to enjoy the fruits of your labors and what will keep you, during those retirement years, in the manner to which you've become accustomed.

But owning equity isn't simply about money; it is also about power. The larger your equity, the greater your influence in the company will be.

There are two ways of acquiring equity. First, you can buy shares of stock outright; second, you can buy options which will allow you to buy stock in the future, or, if the company runs one, you can take part in the stock purchase plan which allows key employees to take part in the company's growth at a somewhat reduced rate.

If you are the chief executive officer, you are in a position to decide the best means for you and your employees to acquire stock. You are the only person, for instance, who can establish a stock purchase plan and, as chief executive officer, you are in a position to acquire more stock than anyone else. From a practical point of view, a stock purchase plan makes good sense—if you allow the loyal deputies you have assembled around you to acquire stock, they will vote with you, giving you a greater control of the company than your own holdings, by themselves, might provide.

Watch Your Public Image

Companies, like movie stars and presidents these days, are much more concerned about their image than they used to be, and the one you should seek to project for your company should reflect its true nature as accurately as possible. Although some Madison Avenue whiz-kid may come up with a superb campaign, your company's image will be determined by its performance and the manner in which it operates, not by a string of self-congratulatory PR handouts. It's difficult these days even to fool some of the people some of the time and they will not believe the claims you make for your company if the facts—the balance sheets, the annual report and so on—tell them something different.

You must be prepared to face up to public criticism on all sorts of fronts—for instance, ecology, consumerism, employment policy toward minority groups. People are infinitely more aware of, and much less willing to see Big Business getting away with misdemeanors, so you must be prepared to listen to criticism and to react accordingly. Presenting the right image to each section of the community can be the deciding factor between success and failure for a company.

4

Getting Started

Now that you are ready to get started, the question uppermost in your mind will be, "Where do I look and how do I go about it?" There is no one sure-fire road to success for a would-be wheeler-dealer. There are many, though they fall roughly into four categories, and each category has its own advantages and opportunities, provided, of course, that you are prepared to seize them.

The High Road—or Large Corporations

The large corporation is by far the easiest and safest road to follow for a novice wheeler-dealer. Since most of us have to work, getting a job within the framework of a large corporation provides a clearly defined path to follow in working your way up to the top.

When selecting a company, consider the type of industry and the services the company performs. Some industries, by their very nature, generate and create opportunities for spectacular growth and development, while others are run along pre-ordained lines, bogged down in red tape and strangled by their own bureaucratic corporate structure. Unless you choose your company carefully, you could be wasting your time. Should you choose wrongly and join a company with an environment that prevents fast movement, you could be a very old man before you arrive at one of the top jobs.

Advertising, publishing, television, motion pictures and certain finance industries are all good examples of areas in which advancement can be rapid. They are highly volatile with high risk and a frequent turnover, but rewards are given for fresh ideas, new techniques and, hopefully, new profits, making them ideal hunting grounds for a wheeler-dealer.

Take the case of Ted Ashley, whose talent agency, Ashley Famous, was acquired by Kinney (later named Warner Communications). After six months, Kinney (parking garages, rent-a-car operations, caskets, etc.) found that in the acquisition of Ashley Famous, they had acquired a major talent, Ted Ashley, who knew the entertainment business not only from an operating point of view but also from the all-important creative side. Having discovered this fine management setup almost by accident, Kinney decided that what they needed now was another company to manage. They set their sights on Warner Brothers-Seven Arts, the acquisition of which changed the entire nature of the original company. So, had you picked Kinney as your place to work in 1969, you

Getting Started

would have been in an ideal spot for a whole range of opportunities from (1) putting together a deal to buy the old Ted Ashley talent agency, which later had to be spun off to avoid a conflict of interests with the movie company; to (2) moving with Ted Ashley himself into what was then an enfeebled movie company to make the big turnaround; or (3) moving into the successfully operated record companies, where more young men have made more large fortunes than in any other single industry.

Another great place to have been in 1975 was Lehman Brothers, a company founded in 1852. Although the company lost some $8 million in 1973 and things were looking bleak, all this changed with the arrival of Pete Peterson, who was eased out of the Nixon Cabinet and who later became chairman of Lehman Brothers. With Lehman in 1975, an employee with new ideas and ambition had to have a great future.

On the other hand, you could have elected to go to work for General Motors or Ford, but auto making is an industry in which it takes patience and longevity to get ahead.

When you are making up your mind about a company, think carefully about its state of development and its prospects for growth because they are crucial in determining your own potential for growth within the organization. Had you joined Polaroid in the mid-1950s, the possibilities, both for you and for the company, were virtually limitless, but if you joined the company in 1975, when the market was already more or less saturated, the prospects would not have been anywhere as good.

Consider very carefully, too, how the corporation is

organized. Is it dominated by one man in the way that ITT is by Harold Geneen, or Gulf + Western by Charles Bluhdorn, or is it like Kodak, basically a bureaucracy which operates through the groups and committees to such an extent that command could change hands at any moment, with no visible alteration to the face of the company at all?

In a personality-dominated organization, your success is directly related to your ability to catch the boss's eye. Not only do you have to make yourself thoroughly familiar with his character and attitudes, and adapt yourself accordingly, but you must also be willing to accept a second-row seat and resign yourself to the never-ending job of putting the boss first, regardless. If you have talent and ambition, then it is almost impossible to play the role of "yes-man" for very long, especially if you don't admire your boss or respect his judgment, but if you have chosen this route, then admiration and respect are the tributes you are expected to pay.

Investigate the company's financing very carefully. Find out as much as you can from the business magazines and newspapers about its debts, its bank loans, the stock situation, shares outstanding, its management and its assets. If it looks sound, go ahead; if it doesn't, then don't—your employment would only be short-term and, unless you are in a position to do something to improve the situation slightly, being associated with a company that collapses won't exactly enhance your reputation.

The level at which you enter a large corporation will depend upon your abilities and experience, and although your education will to some extent determine the

Getting Started

department you will work in, you may still have some choice. If so, then opt for finance rather than sales or marketing, since you are much more likely to come into contact with the people who matter that way. If your training and experience have been in sales or marketing, then set about learning the financial end of the business —accounting especially—as quickly as you can. Having a broad base of knowledge that encompasses both fields will give you an advantage over people with experience in only one. David Mahoney, one of Geneen's alumni and a prime example of how successful the high road can be, started out in advertising, then moved to marketing during his time with ITT, and, after completing his apprenticeship with Good Humor Ice Cream and Colgate, is now president of Norton Simon, a conglomerate which does over $1 billion a year in the hard liquor, soft drinks, magazines and food business. David Mahoney is an example of one person who overlooked the suggested routes to the top of law or finance, and instead chose marketing as his means to success.

In a large corporation, it's unlikely that you will know all your superiors personally, so the only way to attract attention to yourself is through your work. Make quite sure, though, that what you're doing is worth watching because there are always plenty of people only too willing to point out your mistakes.

Lawrence Tisch, like all great wheeler-dealers, has cut out his own particular high road. Admittedly, he got off to a flying start in 1946 with family capital of around $125,000 to launch him and his brother, Bob, in the hotel business, but what he has done with that money in the last thirty years puts him in a class by himself. After thirteen highly successful years spent expanding the hotel business, he moved into movie theaters in 1960 by buying Loew's. Like National General when Gene Klein took over, Loew's had been losing money, but, in eight years, by selling off the unprofitable theaters and spending around $6 million on renovating the rest, Tisch had turned the company around and built considerable assets.

After an unsuccessful attempt to buy into the Commercial Credit Company, an old, staid Baltimore finance company with approximately $3 billion worth of cash, securities and receivables and no desire to do business with a parvenu like Larry Tisch, he turned his attention to the cigarette company, Lorillard Corporation. It seemed an unlikely choice in view of the cancer scare then current and the restrictive advertising regulations, but he believed that all Lorillard needed to resolve its problems was proper management, and time has proved him right.

Now, Tisch has taken on his biggest challenge to date, CNA, the midwestern-based insurance conglomerate. Currently busy firing its management and installing his own people, selling off or closing down its loss-making operations, Tisch will certainly qualify as one of the most successful wheeler-dealers of all times if he makes a success of CNA in the next few years. Tisch is no longer one of the mavericks of the 1960s; he is a new-establishment entrepreneur of the 1970s.

Getting Started

The Low Road—or Small Corporations

As a big fish in a small pond, it is easy to make waves. If you have more than your fair share of intelligence, initiative and drive, you can soon make your presence felt among your superiors. Small companies, by virtue of their size, cannot go in for the same degree of specialization as their larger counterparts, so you may well find that you are expected to fulfill two or more different roles. You will also find that because the company is small and you work in close physical proximity to your colleagues, you will get to know them all personally and will be able to learn about the running of their departments as well as your own. If you make the most of your opportunities, it shouldn't take you too long to learn all there is to know about the running of the company. And, with that breadth of knowledge, you should be able to penetrate the upper ranks of the organization before too long, from where you could either be elected to the top job, or snapped up by a larger organization looking for a well-rounded, versatile executive.

If you choose the low road, the corporation you select is all-important. From a short period spent working in the U.S. headquarters of a foreign car manufacturer, it became very clear that no matter how successful or hardworking an American executive might be, he would not progress beyond a certain level in the company because the parent company wasn't ready to give the top job, or even a vice-presidency, to an American. Unfortunately, some of the talented, loyal American executives had not yet realized that they were, virtually, in a dead-end situation.

So, when you are choosing your company, take a careful look at its promotion policies. See whether any former employees have made it into the top jobs or whether the company usually appoints from the outside. There is no harm in asking what your promotion prospects as an employee might be if the policy isn't clear. It will show that you are ambitious and prepared to make a long-term commitment to the company if the prospects are good, and it will save you wasted years and endless frustration if the prospects are bad.

Saul Steinberg, one of the youngest wheeler-dealers ever—by the time he was thirty-one he had made over $30 million—chose the low road, though he started his small corporation, Leasco, from scratch. In 1962, when the company started, its turnover on sales was only $45,000, but in 1965 he broke into a new field, computer leasing, right at the start of the computer-leasing boom and, having gotten himself a small underwriter, went public for around $1 million. For the next few years, Steinberg was content to expand Leasco. It was a company founded on a single idea, but the timing for that idea was superb and the company grew at a phenomenal rate. It was only when he decided to diversify that he began to meet trouble.

His first major deal in the 1960s—the takeover of the Reliance Insurance Company of Philadelphia—was brilliant, but then his David-and-Goliath tangle with the Chemical Bank in 1969, and later the education he received at Oxford from Robert Maxwell, and his Perga-

Getting Started

mon Press, have left him sadder but wiser, and still very, very rich.

Leonard Schwartz, formerly of the Hudson Vitamin Company, is another prime example of how rewarding the low road can be. When the company went public in 1963, the Brodys, who had founded it years before with two cut-rate drugstores in New York City, decided that they needed a man who understood figures. Schwartz, who was then an accountant at Touche Ross & Company, one of the big eight accounting firms, decided that since he was in no danger of being given a partnership in Touche Ross in less than ten years, he might as well seize the opportunity that Hudson Vitamin was offering. He joined the company, first as controller and later as executive vice-president, and when it became clear to him that there was no obvious heir apparent, he realized that if he learned all there was to learn about the company, from marketing to manufacturing, he could ultimately have the top job. By the time the Brodys were ready to retire, Schwartz was so well versed in the running of the company that he was the obvious choice for the presidency and the job of chief executive officer. When the company was sold to Perfect Film and Chemical Corporation, in 1965, Schwartz, on the Brodys' recommendation, became the key man in the company's expanding operations. With the job came stock options and a substantially increased salary which made Schwartz wealthy enough by 1968 to go out on his own. When last heard of, he owned and was operating a former division of Hudson, selling career apparel through the mail.

In one sense, it could be argued that the legal family

Pritzker from Chicago opted for the low road. It wasn't that A.N., Jack, Jay, Robert and Donald (before his tragic early death in 1972) *worked* for small corporations—they acquired them. "Private" is the adjective most frequently used to describe the Pritzkers. With one exception, their companies are all privately owned. They operate through a series of corporate shells like Refco, Marmon and the GL Corporation—a shell that the family kept on the shelf for so long that by the time they came to use it they'd forgotten what the initials stood for!—and until they bought McCall's from Norton Simon in 1973, nobody outside the network of the deal business had ever heard of them. Although it's a term the family dislikes, they are wheeler-dealers par excellence. They've been described as financial beachcombers, always creating or picking up shell companies invariably when they are in some kind of trouble and the asking price is low. In 1953, for example, Jay and Robert, brothers from the third generation, bought a small caster-making company at a good price from its president, who was anxious to retire. They sold off the unprofitable cycle operation and used what was left as a vehicle to acquire a whole string of other companies—including Marmon, from which the group subsequently took its name—in each case using the same technique of selling off the unprofitable divisions and expanding those that made money. In the case of the Hyatt Corporation, which operates a string of luxury hotels, the family departed from the habits of several generations in that they created the company virtually from scratch and offered the public a chance to participate through a stock offering, though the family

Getting Started

retained over one-third of the common shares. Estimates have placed the family fortune at between $400 million and $1 billion—not bad for a strictly family business.

Another small corporation route is the mom and pop operation, where the son enters the family business with dreams of using all the expensive education which the business has paid for to expand it out of all recognition in a matter of years. The celebrated Dr. Armand Hammer did just that. At eighteen, while he was still at medical school, he was put in charge of the family's small pharmaceutical company by his father and, somehow managing to combine his studies with his business career, was a millionaire before he graduated. Over the next fifty years, he built a multibillion-dollar empire from such diverse activities as selling whiskey, breeding cattle, making billion-dollar deals in fertilizers with the Soviet Union and running Occidental Oil.

It seems to be a popular route. Approximately 85 percent of the Young Presidents' Organization are heads of family businesses, but a more interesting statistic might be the number who are still on speaking terms with Mom and Pop, let alone with the brothers and sisters with whom they had to compete for the key job.

Getting into the family business is easy—your parents will probably be only too delighted to have you—but living with it and getting ahead in it is a very different story. Too many sons have learned the hard way that the frustration, lack of respect and lack of real responsibility that tend to go with the role of heir to the throne are not worth the ultimate rewards. The damage done to a man's self-esteem and initiative during those years of waiting can be irreversible. After years of being downgraded, the self-assurance of youth fades into a lack of confidence and a fear of failure so that, even if the situation is intolerable, the son no longer has the courage to venture into the outside world. So, before you rush into the family business, think carefully. Might it not be a better idea to go and prove yourself in a related field first? Go and work for someone else for a few years and learn as much as you can about their organization so that when you do finally join the family business you have not only valuable experience to offer, but you also have a reputation of your own which will not only put you in a stronger bargaining position with the family, but will also earn you respect from your fellow employees.

Leonard and Ronald Lauder had no such problems with their family business, Estée Lauder. Leonard succeeded his mother as president in 1973. In just under thirty years, the family has built a company worth over $300 million from what was literally a mom and pop operation. Joseph Lauder made up the creams to a formula developed by his wife's uncle, while Estée herself sold them among an ever-growing number of friends and acquaintances. But they soon realized that the big money was to be made by selling through retail outlets such as specialty and department stores, and Estée Lauder, with her almost legendary flair for publicity, soon established the right contacts, starting with the prestigious Saks Fifth Avenue. For almost ten years, in spite of the very glamorous public relations front, the company consisted of Joseph, Estée and Leonard, with Ronald press-ganged into helping his father make the creams after school.

Getting Started

Leonard, however, was a willing volunteer. When he was just sixteen, his parents planned to leave him in charge of the factory while they took a vacation, but he caught chicken pox, so the trip was canceled. He learned the business the hard way. "There isn't a single job in the company that I haven't done," he is quoted as saying in Marylin Bender's book, *At the Top,* "with the exception of the IBM jobs." Neither Leonard nor his younger brother, who joined the company right after college in spite of that initial distaste for making creams, has ever worked anywhere else, and neither would want to. Both now have a degree of independence. Ronald presently runs the Clinique division of the company, while Leonard has charge of the day-to-day affairs of Estée Lauder, though some decisions are still made by his mother. Anything to do with perfume, for instance, still needs her approval in writing. "There's no one who has her nose," her son says by way of explanation.

Estée Lauder is the only major cosmetic company still in private hands—no one outside the family has ever been given a single share—and that's the way they like it. They can run the company their way, without having to worry about pleasing stockholders, and the profits, even split four ways, are more than satisfactory.

Your Own Road—or Starting Your Own Corporation

Whichever road you choose, wheeling and dealing requires tremendous self-confidence and an unshakable belief in your own ideas and abilities, but, if you are going to forge your own road into business and start from scratch, you'll also need a first-class original idea, as well.

The examples that spring most readily to mind are Xerox, originally Haloid (the only asset the company had at the outset was the idea), and the Polaroid camera. Dr. Edwin Land was a gifted scientist who became involved in the problem of the polarization of light while he was doing research at Harvard. In 1937, he set up the Polaroid Corporation to manufacture the polarizing lenses for cameras which he had invented, and although he came up with the Polaroid camera in 1947, it wasn't until the mid-1950s that the idea began to take off commercially. The years before the bonanza, though, were years of uphill struggle. Land was not only faced with the problems of developing his camera but also with raising the finances to market it, which meant trying to convince bankers—those most conservative of men—that the public actually wanted a camera that could develop the photographs it took in ten seconds.

Setting up any company, regardless of the product it is manufacturing or the service it is offering, is such a complicated business from a financial, legal and organizational point of view that the idea of simply buying into an operation that someone else has already set up is understandably attractive.

The legendary Charles Revson was one of the most successful own-roaders of all time. In the early 1930s he, along with one of his brothers and a chemist friend, Charles Lachman, started Revlon with $300 and a new

Getting Started

formula for nail enamel. Today, Revlon is a public company listed on the New York Stock Exchange, with annual sales of over $500 million and yearly profits of around $50 million.

Where Revson was unique was not in his product, but in his marketing methods. While other cosmetic manufacturers sold direct to retail outlets, Revson sold first to beauty salons, and only after the demand was created did he also sell to department stores, drugstores and even supermarkets.

There is no doubt that Revson, himself, *was* the company. He was the creator, the guiding light, chief product manager, marketing strategist and corporate planner. A man who paid the highest salaries in the industry and dangled handsome stock options to lure personnel from his competitors, he was also quick to fire people when they failed to live up to his high expectations. Many executives made fortunes of various sizes as a result of their association with Charles Revson. But when it came to choosing a successor, he went outside the company ranks to fill the post of president and chief executive officer. He selected forty-three-year-old Michel Bergerac, president of ITT-Europe and an executive vice-president of its parent company, whom he lured to Revlon by making him one of the handsomest business propositions known in the corporate world: a five-year contract at $325,000 a year, a $1.5 million lump sum payment to take the position and options for 70,000 shares of common stock at $41 a share. In addition, his transatlantic moving expenses were picked up by the company and he was given a $400,000 buy-back promissory note for his $425,000 New York cooperative apartment.

Mary Wells Lawrence was another "own-roader." In 1966, Mary Wells, as she was then, started her own advertising agency, Wells, Rich, Greene, taking with her from her previous employer, Jack Tinker & Partners, the lucrative Braniff Airlines account. In 1967, she married Harding Lawrence, the president of Braniff Airlines. This was the ultimate ground play; she not only got the account but acquired a husband along the way.

Mary Wells is obviously an advertising genius. Her agency operates with relatively few employees compared to her competitors, but they work harder and receive a higher remuneration for their efforts. And no one works harder than Mary Wells herself. Her main asset is her supreme self-confidence, coupled with an unshakable belief in the rightness of her ideas and in her own abilities. The difference between Mary Wells and thousands of other would-be founders of Madison Avenue agencies is her unique ability to do what so many others *say* they will do.

Riding the crest of the public market in advertising agencies, she set out to create the most exciting ad agency in New York in the 1970s, and she has succeeded. Even her competitors will tell you that, for certain accounts, she provides the best kind of advertising—self-confident and positive. She has that uncanny feeling for what the customer wants, and that alone was enough to get her going in the first place.

Knowing the right people, having the necessary motivation and recognizing the best creative talents helped

Getting Started

her tremendously. Most of all, however, she did what so many others would like to do—she relied on her own instincts, became her own boss and made it.

Other Roads to Travel

A surprising number of wheeler-dealers chose none of the three roads we have described. They didn't start in business at all, but in some other related field. Meshulam Riklis was a stockbroker before he moved into the deal business. Fred Carr was an analyst, and a glance down the *Forbes* list of chief executives will reveal any number of lawyers. What happened was that, after spending some time helping other people make deals and a lot of money, these men realized that they could make deals for themselves at least as well as the people who employed them, if not better. In some cases, they looked for and found their first deal themselves. In others, they were approached by companies that had been impressed by their performance. But whatever the circumstances, there is only one reason for making a major move—to become top man, not to be his attorney or broker or associate—and the first substantial maneuvering comes in getting yourself into a position of real control.

If you are buying into an existing company by acquiring a controlling interest in the stock, then *you* must be the one to negotiate for that position and isolate the broker or lawyer who brought you the deal.

Sometimes, as in my own case, you become a principal in a deal almost by accident. In late 1962, a client by the name of Herb Golden introduced me to the controlling stockholders of Perfect Photo, a company listed on the American Stock Exchange. I attended a meeting at the Four Seasons restaurant in New York with Herb Golden and Karl Hope, the chairman and president of Perfect Photo. I was there in the capacity of attorney, since Herb Golden was my client and had asked me to attend the meeting.

The story that Karl Hope unraveled was a sad one. It seemed that Perfect, a small Philadelphia photo finisher, was in real trouble as a result of too many acquisitions, and so was Mr. Hope. He had taken the company public in the late 1950s, and it was an instant success in the market. The stock was as high as $30 a share until Mr. Hope made a critical mistake; he had a falling-out with his investment banker partners. Shortly after the company had gone public, Hope decided that he wanted to get some money out of his stock and made a deal with a major investment house. They put together a group of pension funds, investment trusts and individual investors who purchased "for investment" (off the market) a substantial block of Perfect's common shares at a price well below the market. Hope, flush with cash, decided to make some other business investments and to expand his personal fixed assets, like a new home.

About this time Karl Hope met a well-known Philadelphia lawyer who advised him that he had been taken to the cleaners, so to speak, by this New York group, who, according to the lawyer, failed to pay Mr. Hope enough money for his stock. What had happened was that shortly after Hope had sold his stock to the New York group, the

Getting Started

price on the American Exchange almost doubled over the price the group had paid Hope. Looking at the newspapers each day, Hope figured out that he had lost a fortune by selling his stock too cheaply. On the advice of counsel, he started a lawsuit which made the front page of the *Wall Street Journal*. It was, alleged Mr. Hope, all a "fraud." The New York group had induced him to sell too cheaply. After considerable litigation expense, the case was settled with Hope getting back his stock and the group getting back their money.

But Karl Hope then had an even bigger problem. Between the settlement and the sale, the Internal Revenue Service determined that Mr. Hope had made a sale of his stock and would have to pay capital gains taxes, which, at the then rate of 25 percent, absorbed a considerable portion of his proceeds from the original sale, as did his other investments. In order to get the necessary funds for the buy-back, he had to borrow from the company's friendly Philadelphia bankers. It all seemed to be working itself out fairly well until Mr. Hope tried to get a refund of his capital gains tax by claiming that the sale was not really a sale but a recision. The IRS said no, and Mr. Hope was left with a substantial loan against his stock.

If the stock price had stayed up, he could have survived, but two things happened which ruined Karl Hope's chances. The company's inner problems started to surface at this time and the angry New York group labeled Karl Hope and his stock a bad risk. It was obvious that he couldn't get away with accusing the group of "fraud" and expect them to support his stock. The market in the stock started to decline from a high of $30 a share to a meager $4 per share in a very short period of time. At $4 per share, and with the company in a decline, the bank started to get very nervous and asked him to repay their loan before it became undermargined.

That was when I met Karl Hope. He was in New York looking for a buyer for his stock and the company. Herb Golden looked like a buyer since he represented several associates who were looking for these kinds of deals. After the initial discussion, Herb Golden and I went to Philadelphia for a meeting with those famous Philadelphia lawyers. On the train, we discussed the deal, and it suddenly became a question of whether it was Herb's deal or my deal. We decided to wait and see what happened in Philadelphia.

When we arrived, matters moved quite rapidly. Hope would sell 300,000 shares of stock and control of the company for $1.2 million—$4 per share—assuming that he could get a commitment and a contract that very day. In order to bind the contract, the sellers wanted $25,000 for a nonrefundable option in order to see if the necessary money could be raised and the deal put together.

The question boiled down to who should put up the money. Herb Golden was there first, but he decided that it was too risky. I could have the deal if I was willing to put up the $25,000 for the option. I suddenly became the lawyer and the principal, with Herb Golden acting as my broker. I put up the $25,000 and then faced the problem of finding the other $1,175,000 in order to avoid losing my $25,000, which was, in itself, borrowed money. That

Getting Started

was how I was initiated into the big leagues of the deal business.

If you plan to go into a new company, then you must ensure that you are the principal promoter by maneuvering yourself into a position of power early on in the game.

If you plan to make your move from the outside, then the law, accounting or investment banking can provide an excellent springboard. Investment bankers are sometimes asked to find a man to take over the management of a company, and many investment banks now have merger and acquisition departments which specialize in setting up deals and finding people to handle them.

When a company runs into trouble, you often find that the company lawyer or accountant is asked to bridge the gap between the departing management and the new regime. Banks and other large-company creditors seem to accept the lawyers and accountants more readily than candidates from either sales or management.

Moving from the role of employee to a position of control can present all kinds of problems, and unless you make sure that you are in a position of real control, you will be fighting a losing battle.

5

The Deal Business

Building Your Own Company: Private vs. Public

Although in many ways it is the toughest means of entry to the deal business, creating your own company from scratch has a lot to recommend it to the would-be wheeler-dealer with no formal business background. What it requires is a great idea and the ability to develop it into a thriving business. All too often, though, these two traits are mutually exclusive—most idea-men do not have the practical businesslike approach needed to exploit their ideas in a really profitable way while the practical businessman does not have the flair and imagination to come up with the all-important ideas in the first place —but when they do coincide in the same individual, the results can be staggeringly successful.

Look at Estée Lauder and Charles Revson, and the millions of dollars they have made. The cosmetics indus-

The Deal Business

try seems particularly suited to ambitious people starting small. You can hardly set up an automobile plant or an investment bank in your own living room with a few hundred dollars' loan, but there is nothing to stop you from mixing face creams in your kitchen and selling them to your neighbors except the Food and Drug Administration.

The first major decision, after having concluded that you are going to put your ideas into action, is do you go private or do you go public? Being a privately owned company means just what the name implies: what you do and how you do it are entirely your own business. Your ultimate responsibility, assuming you stay within the law, is to the stockholders in the company, which means you. In a public company, your responsibility is again to the stockholders, but this time the stockholders are many people, few of whom you will ever know personally. These stockholders range from the ordinary investor to mutual funds, pension funds, banks, trust departments of banks and anyone else who thinks your stock is worth buying. Of course, even though you may be the principal stockholder, owning as much as 80 percent of the company, your primary responsibility is to all of the stockholders, which means that the manner of running the company must be very different from that of a privately run company.

Take the examples of Estée Lauder and Charles Revson once again, both individuals of very strong character who have an innate business sense.

Estée Lauder started as a private company with one single product and built it up to where it is today, a company with about $100 million in annual sales, and it is still a private company. A brilliant businesswoman is Estée Lauder, as everyone will tell you, but a private one. And her ultimate responsibility is to herself and her family, all of whom are involved in the running of the company. Being private, she can gamble on her instincts and launch a high-priced perfume when all the market analysts warn her that the timing is wrong. And when she proves her instincts are right and the professionals are wrong, it is she who reaps the full benefits.

Charles Revson decided on the public route, which required his decisions be made with an eye toward the approval of the board of directors and the stockholders. As president of a public company, Revson's eye was on increased profits and earnings per share because that was what made the stock go up, that's what impressed the bankers and that's what gave him more paper money in the form of stock to make acquisitions or to sell to the public in order to raise more money for new acquisitions.

Up and down the line, the decisions are different if you go private or public.

1. Once the public is admitted to ownership, information must be disclosed. Such information as salaries and your transactions become a matter of public record. Owners of a privately held business often fear that disclosure of such information as sales, profits, competitive position, method of operation and material contracts would place them at a serious competitive disadvantage.

2. By incurring a responsibility to the public, you may lose some flexibility in management. There are practical limitations on salaries and fringe benefits, relatives on

The Deal Business

the payroll and many other day-to-day operating features. Opportunities which might have been personally available to you as the sole owner may have to be turned over to the public, of which you are just a part. The ability to act quickly may be lost to you, especially when approval is required by stockholders and outside directors.

3. There are many additional administrative problems and expenses for a publicly owned company. Routine legal and accounting fees increase substantially. Expenses are incurred for the preparation and distribution of proxy statements and for filing with the Securities and Exchange Commission. There are fees for the transfer of stock, the public relations consultant and, of course, for the time the executives devote to shareholder relations.

4. The owners of a privately held business are often in high tax brackets and prefer that the company pay either no or low dividends, whereas a public company tries to pay the highest dividends possible.

5. A public offering, although providing cash, may be very disadvantageous from an estate tax point of view. The public could value the stock too high or too low, thereby pushing up the estate taxes resulting from your death while leaving the legatees in a noncash position or pushing down the stock to the point where the legatees are left with your losses, making it harder for them to sell the stock to raise money to cover bequests or even living expenses.

6. Once a company is publicly owned, you must consider the inevitable impact of your actions on the price of the stock.

Money, Ego, Power

7. When a significant percentage of your company is owned by stockholders, you can lose control of the company. Once public, you may be forced to dilute your equity to raise additional money, or, because of acquisitions, lose control through a proxy fight or due to a tender offer.

With all of this, most companies that can meet the qualifications do go public. The basic reason is the overwhelming necessity of money to get started or money to move forward. Sometimes, after you have been successful and you decide to go from private to public, you may experience your first blush of wealth. As a private owner, all you have are your shares of the company. Theoretically, the shares are valuable, but you don't actually have the cash in hand to spend, save or squander. By selling out a percentage of your shares in the company—going public—you are acquiring cash in hand.

HOWARD HUGHES—CLASSIC EXAMPLE OF GOING PUBLIC FOR THE CASH

It was impossible to believe that Howard Hughes would ever go public, but there he was in December 1973, selling all of his stock in Hughes Tool Company for $150 million. The private man extraordinary had finally decided to let the public in on his fabled money machine. Since 1924, when he had taken over Houston-based Toolco following his father's death, the company had provided him with a total of over $700 million in before-tax profits. Over the forty-eight years that he

The Deal Business

owned the company, Howard Hughes drained the Toolco money fountain. He may have inherited that trait from his father, whose "take" had always represented a significant fraction of the company's profits.

After his father died in 1924, the young Howard Hughes bought a one-quarter interest that had been left his grandparents and an uncle for $325,000, an investment that soon multiplied many times as a result of the oil boom during the twenties. In the next four years, ending with 1929, the company earned over $20 million before taxes.

Despite its expansion and great success, Hughes Tool managed to retain a family atmosphere; brothers, sons, fathers and uncles all worked for the oil/tool division. Considering his reputation for being cold and insensitive, Hughes enjoyed a remarkably warm relationship with many of his executives in the early years of the company. As his recluse period began, his relationship with his executives also changed, but, according to them, all the stories about his various eccentricities and problems were blown out of all proportion by the press.

There is no question that until December 1973 Hughes Tool was one of the most successful private companies in America. Hughes made all of the decisions and did pretty much what he wanted to do. But by the 1970s he was in trouble financially. Although the value of his assets has sometimes been placed as high as $2.5 billion, knowledgeable observers seem to think he had considerably less than that. A compilation of his known holdings indicates that the total is much closer to $1.2 billion, with many of his assets encumbered by debts.

MONEY, EGO, POWER

Hughes apparently sold his holdings because he needed the cash, and needed it then. It just proves that even with someone as wealthy as Howard Hughes, an extra $150 million is quite important. And the public route seemed the best and the fastest way to raise the money.

In 1973 Hughes sold 100 percent of the company to the public for $150 million. There was only one advantage to Hughes resulting from going public, but, in this instance, the company gained as well—probably more.

1. Hughes obtained $150 million from the offering by selling 100 percent of his equity.

2. Through public ownership of the company, Hughes Tool gained stability, became better known as an independent company and improved its business operations by getting rid of Hughes's interference. In addition, for the first time, other people besides Howard Hughes could become stockholders.

3. Now that Hughes Tool had publicly traded stock, it could contemplate acquisitions and expansion without depleting its own cash or asking Howard Hughes.

4. As a public company, Hughes Tool was better able to attract and retain personnel by offering them equity in the company—a piece of the action in the form of stock which might just make them rich if Hughes Tool continued to grow and gain in profits.

The Deal Business

5. Once the public market was created, assuming that the stock did well, it would be easy to raise additional capital from the public as well as from the institutional investors, who could be solicited on a private basis.

6. Last, but in Hughes's case probably the most important reason of all, it gave Howard Hughes the money when he needed it.

The story of Hughes Tool since going public has been the story of success beyond the dreams of the new stockholders. The oil crisis certainly helped, but probably being freed of Howard Hughes and his image has helped the company gain new business, better management and a greater chance for the future. While it may not have been the best deal for Howard Hughes at that time, it has been very good for those stockholders who took the chance in December 1973.

There are any number of other "going-public" stories —many successful and others not.

Take Saul Steinberg, with his computer leasing company, Leasco, or Larry Spitters, who along with some fellow employees at Ampex decided that he could produce a better and cheaper magnetic tape for computer data—the result was Memorex, one of the hottest stocks of the late 1960s—or even Edwin C. Whitehead and his Auto Analyzer for analyzing blood samples—in 1970 he sold a mere 2.5 percent of his company's stock to the public for millions.

When Mary Wells Lawrence's advertising agency went

public in October 1968, the company's prospectus gave as its reasons for the move the fact that it would be easier to acquire other agencies and to establish stock option and purchase plans "to attract new employees, to offer incentives to key employees and to motivate them to continue in the employ of the company." In 1966, Mary Wells had left Jack Tinker & Partners, taking with her Richard Rich and Stewart Greene—both of whom had been members of the team that created the phenomenally successful "end of the plain plane" campaign for Braniff—and set up Wells, Rich, Greene. When the company was founded, she bought just over 20 percent of the stock—some 30,000 shares—at ten cents a share; when the company went public in 1968, she sold a quarter of those shares at a profit of $1.3 million and then in 1971 sold almost half her remaining shares at a further profit of $2.4 million. Then, in early 1974, when the market for advertising agency stock and most shares in general was way down, she began to buy back shares at a mere $8 or $9 apiece, and in the autumn of that year Wells, Rich, Greene, which by that time *was* Mary Wells Lawrence since both Rich and Greene had gone their separate ways, announced that it intended to go private and buy back about $1.5 million, or 86 percent, of its shares for cash and debentures.

Wells, Rich, Greene was not alone in contemplating a return to its previous private status in view of the general economic climate, but the terms on which it was planning to do so were a little unorthodox, to say the least. For each common share, the company offered $3 in cash and $8 in new ten-year debentures offering 10 percent interest in a year. The offer left the stockholders without any real choice: if they held on, there was only a slim chance that the market would begin to rise again in the foreseeable future and that their stock would regain anything like the price they had paid for it at the crest of the late-1960s wave. If they sold, they would be forced into the position of lending the company money on an unsecured basis, since, as the prospectus revealed, the debentures were very unlikely to fetch even their nominal value on the open market. The deal was heavily criticized. As Commissioner A.S. Sommer of the SEC said in his lecture at the Notre Dame Law School, "The spectacle of entrepreneurs inviting the public in when they can command high prices for their stock and then squeezing them out with little or no practical choice in the matter . . . at substantially reduced prices, is hardly one to warm the soul of Thomas Aquinas or Aristotle."

The reason the company gave for its decision to go private sounded rather similar to those it gave for going public: better opportunities for the company to acquire other companies and to offer employees incentives. The outcome of that offer was that 55 percent of Wells, Rich, Greene is now owned by its directors and officers, of which just over half is in the hands of Mary Wells Lawrence, making her the largest stockholder in the company, and, although profits in 1975 were down from the previous year, she is still an extremely rich lady. The move from private to public revealed her as a very shrewd businesswoman. The return trip suggests that, under that cool, elegant exterior lurks the soul of a real wheeler-dealer.

Money, Ego, Power

H. Ross Perot, allegedly the richest self-made man ever to come out of Texas, probably now wishes that he, too, had made the return trip, after having seen the killing he made by going public in 1968 disappear like water into sand in his subsequent attempts at expansion.

In 1962, he was a salesman with IBM, but what a salesman. By January 19, he had fulfilled his sales quota for the entire year. Not surprisingly, he left IBM soon after and founded his own company, a computer software business called Electronic Data Systems. During the mid-1960s, he managed virtually to sew up the processing of medical insurance claims, and the company grew so rapidly that when he decided to go public in 1968, the 81 percent of the stock that he kept for himself was valued, on paper anyway, at around $1.5 billion. It was, as *Fortune* said, "perhaps the most spectacular personal coup in the history of American business."

Finding himself in the big league, Perot, like other wheeler-dealers before and since, sought to make acquisitions that would bring him not only more money but also prestige and acceptance by the business and financial establishment. So, in 1970 he bought the old respectable Wall Street firm of duPont, Glore, Forgan & Company. To Perot, it was a foot in the door. If he could introduce his modern, computerized methods into duPont's back office successfully, then the whole of Wall Street, almost deliberately behind the technological times, would be his oyster.

His excitement at the potential opportunities, not surprisingly, led him to underestimate the problems that duPont was facing when he took over, and when the

The Deal Business

realization did dawn he continued to pour money into the company. Perot did this partly because he, like a good many other people on Wall Street, believed that the crisis was only temporary, and also because he knew that if duPont went under, his opportunity to be the cybernetic savior of Wall Street would be gone forever. In the two years that followed, he spent an estimated $85 million and still failed to turn duPont around. Even the acquisition of Walston, another Wall Street firm, and the forming of two new companies, duPont Walston and duPont, Glore, Forgan, failed to stop the rot.

In January 1974, the board of duPont Walston voted to liquidate. In addition, stock in Electronic Data Systems, Perot's goose that laid the golden eggs, took a sharp knock after the revelation that many of the company's Medicare contracts had been won through friendship with members of the Nixon administration and that their renewal, therefore, was in considerable doubt. To cap it all, in July 1975, the bankruptcy trustees of duPont Walston filed a suit against Perot, seeking $45 million in actual damages and a further $45 million in punitive damages.

Perot's mistake was not in going public per se—$1.5 billion can hardly be called a mistake under any circumstances—but in not staying where he was or getting out when the going was good. In other words, had Perot not believed that he could turn around duPont, Glore, Forgan and Company, he would have remained one of the most successful wheeler-dealers of the 1960s. Timing is everything to the wheeler-dealer, and Perot lost his timing in the 1970s.

Money, Ego, Power

Acquiring a Vehicle

Acquiring a suitable vehicle—a company that, for one reason or another, is ripe for takeover and reorganization—is the dream of most wheeler-dealers, and for obvious reasons. You are acquiring a going concern with an administrative, legal and financial structure, certain assets or good will, or even both, which provides a ready-made shell within which the company you envisage can grow.

The vehicle you choose may be a small private company like those advertised in the *Wall Street Journal* or an unsuccessful public corporation of any size which has failed to fulfill its primary reason for existing. The most desirable vehicle is the public company, one with some public ownership, low-priced stock (usually sold in the over-the-counter market, but possibly listed on some stock exchange) and some assets including tax-loss carry forwards, though they inevitably mean some liabilities and creditor problems, too. Ideally, you should be able to gain control of the board of directors with the purchase of only a small amount of stock and that at a relatively nominal price or with the extensive use of leverage. If you are looking for a suitable vehicle, then the people to ask are brokers, investment bankers or merchant bankers, who will know which companies are on the market and any relevant financial details. Also, check the advertisements in the financial newspapers, which are always a great source for vehicles.

One of the notable success stories in this field is that of Meshulam Riklis and Rapid Electrotype, which

The Deal Business

formed the basis for Rapid American, his giant corporation which, at one stage in the early 1970s, was the third most profitable company in the United States. And then there is Charles Bluhdorn, who moved out of commodities and into a small auto-parts company now called Gulf + Western. As a reporter remarked after a stockholders' meeting recently, "Can you buy anything these days that isn't made by Gulf + Western?" And there's Gene Klein with his National General Corporation. . . . The list is endless.

Turning Around a Company in Trouble

Of all the ways of getting into the deal business, trying to turn around a company in trouble carries the highest rewards in terms of both money and ego gratification—and, also, carries the highest risks. The would-be wheeler-dealer who attempts it must have not merely courage, but also very special qualities and qualifications. He must have a first-class reputation in the business and the financial world, and his level of preparation must be such that he can grasp fully the nature of the problems he has to try to solve. He must not allow sentiment to influence his judgment in any way. He must move fast to fill a vacuum, and if that means moving in on old friends and associates, then he must do it. He must also have supreme self-confidence in order to convince the company's creditors—often those most cautious of institutions, the banks—that he knows precisely what he is doing, and he must have guts.

Money, Ego, Power

A company in trouble is no place for a man who is gun-shy, but it is equally worth remembering that discretion is the better part of valor and that, while it is the supreme ego trip to move in where chaos reigns and where other people have failed, you must nevertheless look extremely carefully at the situation into which you are moving. It might be that no matter how talented and courageous you are, the problems that particular company is facing might be too great for *anyone* to overcome. And even if it is of some consolation to you to know that, as you lick your wounds, the rest of the business community will make no allowances. A failure is a failure, no matter how greatly the odds were stacked against you in the first place. Admittedly, it is impossible to protect yourself totally against the risk of failure, but you can minimize that risk. Never move in unless you are sure, first, that you can take full command, either by controlling the board or by presenting a plan in advance which is accepted unanimously by the board with guarantees that it will be carried out, and second, that you have the full support of the company's creditors, especially the banks, because without it you have no chance of success.

It is essential to negotiate your position and powers in advance. While you are still outside the company, you are potentially its savior and, therefore, in a much stronger bargaining position than you will be once you are an employee.

If, once you have joined the company, you find that your powers are being restricted or if a move you consider essential for the survival of the company is opposed by the board, then resign. If the captain of the *Titanic* had wanted to change course *before* the collision and had been prevented from doing so by his officers, then no glory would have accrued to him for going down with his ship.

HERB ENGELHARDT AT BECK

The story of Herb Engelhardt's time at Beck Industries shows only too clearly the pitfalls to avoid. When Beck hit serious trouble in 1970, both Newton Gleckel and Chuck McDevitt resigned, and a caretaker president and chairman, Manny Rothberg, who led the preferred stockholders group and who had worked a minor miracle with W. & J. Sloane in Los Angeles, was appointed to hold the fort.

At that stage the prognosis for Beck, in spite of the mammoth problems it faced, was good. The company's creditors were in a mood to try and save the company, the banks had advanced an additional $5 million, and the opportunity to turn Beck around was ripe. Although Rothberg had the experience to handle Beck's problems, he was a sick man and needed someone younger and stronger to do the actual work.

Enter Herb Engelhardt, an associate of John Loeb at Loeb Rhodes & Company, with extensive experience— and considerable success—in straightening out companies in financial difficulty. A few years earlier, Engelhardt could have taken his pick of any number of top jobs, but he had waited perhaps just a little too long to make his move so that when the job at Beck came along, he jumped at it without fully considering either the problems of the company or his own position within it.

Unlike Gleckel and McDevitt, Engelhardt had little to start with. The company's stock had been delisted from the American Stock Exchange, its credit was no longer good, its operations were making a substantial loss, and perhaps most serious of all the power of the board had been rapidly diminished. It was now loaded with members who were stock- or noteholders, who had sold their companies to Beck during McDevitt's spending spree and whose primary concern, not unnaturally, was with their own position and not with the company as a whole.

Engelhardt tried to establish himself as an independent force, but he had no real power. Having been installed by Manny Rothberg and the Sloane group, he was viewed with suspicion by all the other factions and was looked on by the group who had sponsored his appointment as their man, their employee, not as the independent chief of Beck. Englehardt's major mistake was in being too eager to take the job. Had he insisted on control of the board, had he gained the backing of the banks as the *sole* man responsible, had he been willing to make enemies of the people who had sponsored him—if there was no other way of achieving what he believed had to be achieved—then he might have been able to save Beck from bankruptcy. But under the conditions Engelhardt accepted at Beck, the task was an impossible one.

The company filed for a Chapter XI reorganization under the bankruptcy laws, and Engelhardt, with an undeserved blot on his reputation, left to find a new way to make a living.

The Deal Business

ACKERMAN AT CURTIS

And then—to come down to firsthand experience—there was the Curtis Publishing Company, which published *Ladies' Home Journal, Holiday, American Home* and, of course, *The Saturday Evening Post*. In 1968, the company was in deep trouble. Although only eight years earlier it had been making a profit of around $9 million, it was then producing a staggering $62 million loss, almost half of which had been spent on trying to keep the ailing *Saturday Evening Post* alive.

What precipitated the crisis at Curtis in March 1968 was that the banks to which Curtis owed millions of dollars announced that, unless the management of the company was replaced, they would call in the loans.

The more I looked at Curtis, the more I realized it was the biggest, sickest company I had ever seen, but, even so, I believed it could be turned around. On April 22, the board at Curtis accepted an offer made by my company, Perfect Film and Chemical, under which we would loan Curtis $5 million, to persuade the banks to extend their loans, and I would become president and chief executive officer of the company to see whether a merger between Curtis and Perfect was possible. Once I arrived at Curtis, it became abundantly clear that the company was not in a strong enough position to merge with Perfect or anyone else, and that the best we could hope for was to avoid bankruptcy and create a shell company, with cash and other liquid assets, plus a large, healthy tax-loss carry forward—in short, to build an almost ideal vehicle, but for somebody else, not me.

Money, Ego, Power

The basic problem with Curtis, or so it seemed to me, was that it saw itself as a manufacturing company—in the paper business, the printing business, the circulation business—and looked on publishing as merely a spinoff of all these other activities, an attitude which, over the years, had created a serious problem for the magazines.

Suppose *Ladies' Home Journal* had decided to change the quality of its paper and the size of its pages to cut costs and had been dealing with independent paper suppliers and printers. It could simply have stated its new requirements, and if the firms concerned could not meet them, then it could have taken its business elsewhere. Under the setup at Curtis (one of the only firms, as *Time* put it, to start with trees and end up with magazines), if the paper-making division couldn't produce the new desired quality of paper and the printing plant couldn't handle the new size, the *Ladies' Home Journal* had to remain unchanged. This was an example of vertical integration at its worst.

The one hope for Curtis, I believed, was subdivision. In the same way that Jimmy Ling had divided Wilson Sporting Goods and Wilson Pharmaceuticals into two totally separate entities, I thought that Curtis, like Gaul, should be divided into three parts—publishing, printing and paper-making—each of which could be merged with the other companies which had similar interests, in a stock deal.

But the most pressing problem was the magazines. *Ladies' Home Journal,* prestigious though it was, was costing the company around $9 million a year; so in early summer 1968 it was sold to Downe Communications,

The Deal Business

along with *American Home,* and freed from the stranglehold of the Curtis printing and paper-making divisions. Both are still flourishing and profitable today.

But *The Saturday Evening Post* remained the biggest headache of all. Over the next seven months, we tried almost everything we could think of to save it: the subscription list was cut in half, we concentrated on the A and B advertising categories, and made the magazine itself more sophisticated, but by January 1969, after the magazine had lost almost $7 million in the nine months since I had taken over, it became painfully clear that continuing publication was no longer a viable proposition.

There were howls of protest from many different quarters: *The Post* was an American institution; how could it be allowed to die? Books were even written, casting me in the villain's role. And the fact that when I left Curtis in the spring of 1969 the Curtis Publishing Company was still alive, *Holiday* and *Ladies' Home Journal* were still alive, the creditors had all been paid and the danger of bankruptcy, which at one stage had been a very real possibility, had been averted, has tended to be overlooked.

But that is not to say that I believe my time at Curtis was a success. When I took over, my aim had been to turn the company—*The Saturday Evening Post* and all—around, and, clearly, I had not achieved that aim. With the advantage of hindsight, I believe that Curtis's problems were just too great to solve without sacrificing *The Post*. By the mid-1960s, the days of the mass-circulation general magazine were over. Television had cornered that market, not merely as a medium of news and information but also of advertising, and the only real hope for magazines was in the specialist field. Look at the success now of publications like *Psychology Today*, *Fortune* and *New York*. The days of *The Saturday Evening Post* were numbered before I arrived. My mistake was in not realizing it.

The Sell-out and the Buy-in

Perhaps the safest entry into the deal business—"safe" being a comparative term, since the last thing wheeling and dealing offers is job security—is either the sell-out or the buy-in, or acquisition. If you have made a success of your own small company but have decided that what you really want now is financial security, then selling out to a larger or simply more ambitious company might well be the answer. Unless you take the money and run, what happens in effect is that you become a partner in the new enterprise, and the role you play within it is very much up to you. If you simply want a quiet life, then you can become virtually a sleeping partner, but if you are ambitious, then it can be a means of entry into the big time. Instead of being chief stockholder and chief executive of one small company, you become a partner in a larger venture or even a string of ventures, from where you can maneuver yourself into the top job.

Sometimes the sell-out can lead to your developing new talents or employing the old ones in a new way. Look at Louis Harris of Harris Poll fame. He sold out to the aggressive go-ahead investment house of Donaldson Lufkin Jenrette, the first securities firm to go public.

The Deal Business

They decided to use Harris's skills in determining how people would buy and sell securities.

As an ambitious wheeler-dealer, the buy-in, or acquiring of other companies, is likely to be of more interest to you than the sell-out, and the last few years have been a very good time for it. During the go-go years of the 1960s, it was almost impossible for a private company to find another private company ripe for acquisition—the competition from the big companies was too great. Following the deconglomeration trend of the early 1970s, suddenly there were plenty of suitable companies on the market, as the big conglomerates begin to offload the acquisitions they had made when the market was high and which they found they could not handle when the market began to fall.

With all those bargains on the market, tempting though it is simply to rush out and buy, you should decide exactly what you are trying to do and what your goals are over the next ten years, say, before you make a move. Look first at the company you already have—the one that will become the parent company—and ask yourself if it has a suitable management structure which can absorb the running of the other companies, or is it essentially a small company and should it stay that way. Think very carefully, also, about how you make your acquisitions. You may be tempted to acquire a company with a small amount of cash plus a contract offering the seller a high salary for the next five years and leasing the buildings he owns from him on a yearly basis, too. Admittedly, it means you have to find much less cash than if you were buying the company outright. It also means that, since you are committed to those buildings, you cannot centralize your operations or find bigger, more effective premises, and, unless you are prepared to pay off the seller's contract, you won't be able to hire a more efficient man to run the business for you.

Before you even think about making a deal, you must understand why the seller is selling. If he is getting old and wants to retire or wants the financial security of a large amount of cash in the bank, fine, but if he wants to take stock instead and stay in the company, make sure you understand the nature of the man you are dealing with. If he is insecure, then he is going to be knocking on your door every time the stock goes down a point or two, so you must tailor the deal to suit him very carefully or you will have a real problem.

A good example of the first case was the takeover of Hudson National by my company, Perfect Film and Chemical, in 1965. The three founding partners of the company wanted to retire and were prepared to sell the company outright for $6 million in cash. The first thing we did was to examine the middle management very carefully to see whether the company would survive without its three key men, since it required a lot of technical know-how. (It was not the sort of company that could be run successfully by any bright young man straight out of the Harvard Business School.) The deal went ahead with all sides understanding exactly why Hudson National was being sold. The air was clear, and since the partners were all retiring on the day the deal went through, the executives who were left realized there was an excellent opportunity for promotion and, there-

The Deal Business

fore, gave the deal their backing. Had the partners stayed on for a year or two, the middle management, in whose hands the success of Hudson lay, might have got discouraged and looked for jobs elsewhere.

That is not to say, though, that a deal cannot succeed if the seller continues to work for the company. Take the example of a small professional photofinishing company we acquired in 1963. The seller was basically a sales and marketing man with no real knowledge of accounting and no administrative background who wanted someone to take care of that side of the operation, along with some financial security and a job in which he could take some pride. Perfect was able to provide the things he lacked—systems, budgets, controls—and in less than five years the company increased its profits manyfold, with the seller still running the company and doing a more effective job than he had been doing when we bought the company.

One final point to bear in mind: A company's decision to sell is almost never made overnight, so that during the period when the members of the board have been considering the move, they will have been conserving cash rather than reinvesting in the company. When you are thinking about the price, you must take into account the missing investment, which you will have to make up immediately when you take control. So, although Hudson National's asking price was $6 million, it was effectively nearer $9 million, since the company needed an investment of $3 million immediately.

The story of my first few years at Perfect is an example of how all these buy-in problems come together. Having

MONEY, EGO, POWER

acquired control of Perfect in 1962 for $1.2 million, I became chairman and president of a company on the American Stock Exchange. I had made the acquisition with a very inadequate investigation of the company, and when I arrived in my new position, I found a company that was suffering from a massive case of "corporate indigestion." In a period of three years, the company had acquired some thirty different companies, each of which was, in the main, a small regional photofinisher. These companies were amalgamated, merged and acquired. Perfect used every technique known in business—from the purchase of assets to the pooling of interests, acquisitions for stock and so forth—to pull these companies together.

By 1962, when I took over, there were grave problems. While the acquisitions looked sound on the surface, they were never soundly conceived nor soundly executed. The business philosophy of the company—to go from regional to national photofinishers—made a lot of sense, but management was unable to handle the inherent problems of the changeover.

The parent company, itself a small regional photofinisher, did not have sufficient management depth to help organize and manage the companies acquired. Generally, the acquisitions had mom and pop bookkeeping systems, regionally oriented policies and small-company business methods. The problem became one of amalgamating these acquisitions with the parent company to produce one cohesive company rather than thirty separate entities. And the questions that arose centered around the costs involved in the amalgamation and

The Deal Business

whether or not the companies should have been acquired at all without the necessary personnel to handle the acquisitions.

If you want to have a successful buy-in program, all of these questions, and more, have to be asked and answered before you buy, not afterward when it's too late.

GRASSIE AT BECK

The supreme recent example of the buy-in—had it actually come off—would have been Frank Grassie's attempts to take over Beck Industries when it got into serious trouble.

As vice-president at U.S. Shoe, Grassie had tried to buy Beck's unprofitable retail footwear division which everyone was only too eager to unload when Chuck McDevitt's overambitious acquisition program landed the company in serious financial difficulty. When the proposed deal fell afoul of the antitrust laws, Grassie got permission from his former employers to explore the deal on his own. He was not concerned with the stores' past retail records—he looked on them merely as parcels of real estate located in some of the country's best shopping centers. He made an offer of around $11 million, convinced that he could make the company profitable by 1971 by closing down some of the stores and converting the rest to shoe boutiques and specialty stores concentrating on high-priced ladies' shoes. There was only one problem. Grassie had no money. The chairman of Beck, Manny Rothberg, was impressed by Grassie and offered him a job, but Grassie turned it down and, instead, managed to raise $2 million for the down payment from investors in his adopted hometown of Cincinnati. In the end, though, he didn't use the money; to have done so would have meant yielding control of the company he was about to buy to his backers, and he saw no future in that. So, he went to Beck and offered to assume their debts up to the value he had placed on the company—around $11 million—in exchange for the company. Beck, or at least the faction led by Manny Rothberg, was by this time clutching at straws and wanted to accept the offer, but the final word lay with the banks from which Beck had borrowed heavily to finance its own buy-in program and which were the company's chief creditors.

Having talked to Grassie, the banks, normally the most cautious of institutions, decided to take a chance and also accepted his offer, but before the details could be finalized, Beck filed for a Chapter XI reorganization under the bankruptcy laws and the deal fell through. Had Grassie managed to pull it off, it would have been the ultimate in wheeling and dealing; he would have gained control of a major company without it having cost him a penny.

Growth by Merger

If you look at the deal business, you will find that probably every company has, at one time or another, accelerated its growth or expansion by way of merger. Whether you start by building your own company from scratch, acquire a vehicle, turn a company around or put

The Deal Business

a group together, somewhere along the line you will consider a merger for expansion. Understanding the basics of this kind of expansion is essential to an understanding of the deal business.

VERTICAL MERGERS

A vertical merger is expansion by integrating the successive stages of production—backward toward the raw material or forward toward the consumer. If you sell cosmetics, then why not buy a company that manufactures the products which go into the cosmetics? Of course, vertical mergers can be quite a dangerous proposition because a company can lose the flexibility of alternative sources as conditions change.

One of the most vertically integrated companies of the late 1940s and early 1950s was the Curtis Publishing Company, which, as we saw earlier in the chapter, was too vertical. By starting with the trees in the forests of Maine, making paper in Pennsylvania and printing in Philadelphia, Curtis thought it was in great shape. During the Second World War and immediately afterward, this was probably true, but once alternative sources of paper and printing became available, Curtis was locked into one kind of paper from its paper-making plant and one size of printing from its printing plant in Philadelphia. When it became necessary to reduce the size of its magazines to save money, Curtis just couldn't move to a smaller-size format like its competitors. For Curtis, vertical integration was a disaster. Had it not owned its successive stages of production, it would have maintained the flexibility needed to remain competitive. Vertical mergers may be good, but you should consider quite clearly whether, in the long run, it's not better to have the other stages of production owned by someone else, so that you can bargain with them or change if your competitive situation changes.

HORIZONTAL MERGERS

The horizontal merger is one that combines companies engaged in the same stage of production, and it is frequently entered to extend the geographic scope of the market coverage or perhaps to develop a broader line of similar products. The value of this kind of merger is that it capitalizes on present market skills and is particularly attractive from a competitive point of view. Of course, you must bear in mind antitrust legislation, and, also, the reality of combining two organizations often may not mean that you will get the results you hoped for. But expanding horizontally is still, by far, one of the best reasons to merge or acquire.

THE CONGLOMERATE

Conglomerate expansion, also called economic diversification—or the "shotgun approach"—involves the acquisition of firms whose products bear little relation to those of the acquiring firm. Conglomerate acquisition

The Deal Business

may be the fastest way to establish a foothold in growth areas or provide a quick broadening of the production base, but at the same time the probability of success is diminished by the increased risk that is associated with operating in a number of different industries. Conglomerates have been pioneered by many of the wheeler-dealers mentioned in this book because, for most of them, it represented the fastest way to grow. However, since market performance is the ultimate goal, and this performance is based upon corporate profit, most of the conglomerate mergers have been sheer disasters.

Of course, as most wheeler-dealers have learned, putting two companies together means more than adding the two profit statements. In looking for their acquisitions, the men in a hurry took the easiest way first. Those who were willing to sell, sold for a good reason, the reason usually being that they were not as profitable as their competition, which is why they were up for sale at an attractive price. This is where the conglomerate got its start. At the beginning, it looked to the wheeler-dealers like a rather easy game to play. And there was never any shortage of players.

Stockholders also became convinced that everybody automatically made money out of mergers. The mere announcement of a conglomerate merger was enough to move a stock up four or five points. The spirit of adventure generated by the acquisition game made it the most exciting game in town. Everyone wanted to play. As *Fortune* put it, "The chief executive who leads his company through these engagements sees himself as the protagonist of an exciting drama." The ego of the players became as important as the game they were playing. There are, clearly, good and bad conglomerates, but what the history of the 1960s has taught us is that just to acquire is not enough; the reason for conglomeration must make good business sense or it will surely fail. Ask Jim Ling. (See Jim Ling's story in chapter 6.)

CONCENTRIC

What has been called concentric expansion may be less an expansion strategy than a general management philosophy. At any rate, concentric expansion involves locating the company's strengths—whether these be management skills, marketing knowledge or production abilities—and setting out areas of diminishing strength around the core. For example, an aerospace firm with outstanding system-management ability as its nucleus and with good electronic capability but poor consumer marketing experience may elect to develop a totally automated system package, such as an advanced materials handling system. The expansion, then, is toward the company's strength and away from its weakness.

The choice, then, in growth by merger is based upon what you hope to accomplish. Remember, though, that there is no ideal acquisition or merger. The perfect firm does not exist, and if it did, it certainly would not be for sale at a price that would make it worthwhile for your company to buy. As a practical matter, what will be avail-

The Deal Business

able will always have defects; it's whether or not you can correct the company's defects that becomes the key to success or failure.

Putting a Group Together

The wheeler-dealer is by nature a solitary animal. He needs other people to work with him, admittedly, but when it comes to the crunch he is the only one to call the shots and make the key decisions. There are exceptions though, and the most notable among them is Donald Parsons. But perhaps what happened to him and the group he put together illustrates very clearly that it is the exception that proves the rule.

THE PARSONS GROUP

In 1963, Donald Parsons, a prosperous thirty-three-year-old Detroit lawyer, set the staid Michigan banking fraternity on its ear by getting together a group of like-minded businessmen and launching what was then an unprecedented razzle-dazzle proxy fight for control of Detroit's fourth largest bank, the $486 million Bank of the Commonwealth.

The Parsons group, which was causing all the trouble, consisted of about thirty businessmen in their late thirties and forties—the oldest among them was fifty-one—who shared common backgrounds, strong school ties and memberships in the same clubs, and had abundant family wealth and a very healthy desire to make even more money. They had bought around one-third of the Bank of the Commonwealth's stock for $23 million, and, less than seventy-two hours after launching the proxy fight, they had control of the bank and were into the big time.

Flushed with success and taking an almost schoolboyish delight in the fact that it was shaking up Michigan's long-established financial community, the group moved from bank to bank, always operating within the law and with some flair, and financing the purchases with loans from other banks—not those it had already bought but others, from banks that wanted their corresponding bank deposits. But, then, in 1969, Parsons began to hit trouble. Like so many other wheeler-dealers who had used high leverage to finance his acquisitions, he suddenly found that money was tight and also that he was in trouble with the federal authorities, who, it was said at the time, had only been waiting for him to make his first slip.

The earnings of his banks started to slide and the loan reserves went up from bad debts. He found himself in a liquidity crisis, first at his banks because of high interest rates in the market, then later because there was no market for his long-term securities as the rates kept climbing. Then, as the price of his bank stocks tumbled, he found himself in a personal liquidity crisis, too. The final straw came when the Federal Reserve let it be known that it wanted the Parsons group out of banking. The group got out, having lost a lot of money, and Parsons is once again practicing law.

The Deal Business

Undoubtedly, Parsons would have been better off without his group. Had he gone into the deal business on his own, he would not have been able to make such spectacular deals and would almost certainly have been left with something, instead of nothing, at the end of it all. The essence of wheeling and dealing is speed; you need to act quickly, and if you have to consult not one or two but thirty partners every time, it may take you hours, even days, instead of minutes to reach important decisions. And with thirty partners, there are bound to be clashes of personality and conflicts of interest, which again are not conducive to the free-wheeling, spur-of-the-moment style which most top players in the deal game display.

You cannot, as the Parsons group proved conclusively, wheel and deal by committees.

Second Man to the Leader

Wheeler dealers and great comedians have one thing in common—an impeccable sense of timing. In the case of wheeler-dealers, timing means knowing not only when to make a move, but also how to be in the right place at the right time. The right place can be as second man to the leader, and the right time can be when the company hits trouble.

Although companies, and banks to whom the task of finding a new broom to clear up the mess often falls, still do go outside the company for a new leader, a good second man on the spot will usually be given the first chance. There is, however, always the danger that if you have been the second man for too long, you may be considered a born Number Two and, therefore, won't be given first crack at the top job. But if you are passed over by your own company, which prefers to go outside, then you may well be exactly what another company is looking for if it chooses to ignore its second man, too.

SANDY SIGOLOFF AT REPUBLIC

Sandy Sigoloff's timing was perfect. First, he joined Xerox when the company was expanding at a phenomenal rate and, by the mid-1960s had become a company vice-president in charge of the Electro Optical Systems division. In 1968, he was invited by a personal friend of many years' standing, Gerald Block, to join his Republic Corporation. Republic was one of the high-flying Beverly-Hills-based conglomerates of the 1960s, and its stock when Block took over had been showing a deficit of 12 cents per share, but by 1967 was earning around $2.

Sigoloff declined Block's offer, but, realizing that the bonanza period at Xerox was coming to an end—in the Electro Optical Systems division anyway—left the company. He teamed up with venture analyst Fred Carr to form a new company, but it did not get off the ground. When Block repeated his offer in 1970, Sigoloff did not refuse. It wasn't simply that Sigoloff needed a job; the situation at Republic had changed dramatically in the intervening two years. The recession had hit Block's dozens of tiny unrelated companies hard, and he desperately needed help. In October 1970, Sigoloff became senior vice-president and trouble-shooter at Republic. In December, he was elected president and chief operating officer, and, almost immediately, came the bad news that Republic was on the verge of bankruptcy and was fighting for its life, and, with it, the announcement that Sigoloff, having spent only a matter of weeks as second man, was the new boss and Block was out.

Immediately, Sigoloff set about dismantling the empire his predecessor and benefactor had created. Many of the companies were sold off or closed down as he concentrated on the highly lucrative film processing and steel products divisions. And, perhaps most important, he managed to hammer out a deal with the banks extending Republic's loans, thus giving it the time it needed to stage a recovery. Over the next few years, Sigoloff consolidated the company's position and, by 1973, considering that the job he set out to do had been satisfactorily completed, he moved on, ultimately ending up as president of Daylin's, a big Los Angeles drugstore chain. This time he moved in as top man.

Jim Slater, Born Wheeler-Dealer

If you wanted to pick one man whose actions exemplified every technique indigenous to the wheeler-dealer, it would have to be James D. Slater. To England, Jim Slater was a combination of Gerry Tsai, Jimmy Ling, Saul Steinberg, Larry Tisch, Charles Bluhdorn and Meshulam Riklis, all rolled into one. Slater Walker, in its various forms, was a conglomerate, bank, mutual fund, real estate and insurance company, and entrepreneur extraordinary to English business. It spawned dozens of subsidiaries and satellites, which were sold, liquidated and spun off, all to satisfy Jim Slater's drive to get to the top of the top.

Unlike many of the entrepreneurs who control so much of the business in "the City," as London's financial center is known, Jim Slater was not a member of the usually impenetrable "old-boy network" of private school (in England, they are called public schools) graduates. The son of a small contractor, he left school at sixteen, trained as an accountant and qualified at age twenty-four. In the 1960s, with his modest savings of £2000, he got interested in the stock market, and, before long, he was £50,000 richer. In 1963, he met Peter Walker, a member of Parliament and a man of similar age and background, who became his partner. Together, they started Slater Walker, and English business has not been the same since.

Their company was uniquely British and would not have adapted successfully in America to the New York Stock Exchange. For example, there is no law in Britain that requires banks to separate their commercial banking from their trust operations, and there is no legislation prohibiting inside trading, Securities and Exchange Commission style. In England, insider trading and self-dealing are accepted courses of action. Going public takes on a different connotation, as do bids and deals, which in the United States would be called mergers and acquisitions. To confuse the situation further, regula-

The Deal Business

tions are not always the same for everyone—a great deal depends on who you are and who your friends are, and whether the City's old-boy network thinks you are good or bad for its reputation.

There is no question but that British business had a love/hate relationship with Jim Slater. Some people believed he was the best thing to happen to British merchant banking in one hundred years, while others thought he was a darling of the press but would never be accepted by the City establishment—a group that makes the Union League Club members look like a bunch of swingers—and would eventually receive their chastisement.

What Slater did best was to reorganize old companies which had capital but no management and no growth. He was called an "asset stripper of the first magnitude." His first acquisition was a clothing manufacturer that he bought for a price under its book value, and then he promptly sold its main asset, an office building. From then on, it was a similar pattern: buying companies at less than their book values, selling off the parts and investing the profits from the sales into new acquisitions. This was a typical pattern followed by American wheeler-dealers, but in England, where old-style companies seem to prefer sitting with their losses to making waves by selling assets and cutting losses, this was revolutionary.

To grow even faster, Slater sought to generate interest in his shares, which, in turn, were used to make more acquisitions—again, a typically American conglomerate pattern. The press loved him and the challenge that he represented to the old-boy network. They also loved him because he was the living denial of the accepted wisdom that British industry is lazy, unproductive and poorly managed. Slater's mere presence on the English business scene was enough to provoke many companies into growth just to avoid the clutches of Slater Walker.

As invariably happens on the way to the top, Slater discovered that banking, insurance and money deals generally are better than any manufacturing company, with all of its inherent capital and employment problems. In the mid-1970s, he started to liquidate into cash, selling almost anything that would bring a decent price. These sales probably saved Slater Walker from the fate of its competitors in the fringe banking industry. In 1973, he tried for the big bail-out in attempting to merge with old and established Hill, Samuel, the biggest merchant bank in the City and the one with the least conservative image. At the last moment, however, the deal broke up and Slater was on his way down.

In late 1975, Jim Slater resigned from Slater Walker, turning the company over to his good friend Jimmy Goldsmith, another forty-two-year-old wheeler-dealer. Jim Slater's desire to get out was so important to the Bank of England, which already feared a crisis of confidence, that the central bank's governor, Gordon Richardson, played a major role in orchestrating his exit from the English business scene. When he resigned, Jim Slater said that he planned to spend more time with his wife and four children, enjoying his life. His position on the English business scene would have been a difficult one for anyone to hold, let alone the quiet, family-oriented Slater, who was not part of the inner network. The ma-

The Deal Business

chinations of this closed group cannot be underestimated, and unlike in America, in the City, where a man is judged not so much on his accomplishments and success but first on his background, schooling and social position, being a self-made brilliant success is regarded as almost unsportsmanlike.

6

What Not to Do

We have talked a lot about successful wheeler-dealers, men who played the game and came out on top. But it would be unrealistic to suggest that the deal business is like a children's party game, with prizes for everyone. A considerable number of those who try their hand fail. Some, like Saul Steinberg, lose just one battle; others, like Jim Ling, lose the whole war.

For every success, there have been at least one hundred or more failures. It is clear that a common psychological trait of all wheeler-dealers, both the successful and unsuccessful ones, is their willingness to take great risks—some for more money, others simply for ego. All of the men and women mentioned in this book share a common conviction that, to make a lot of money, to satisfy their ego or to acquire power, they must take enormous business risks.

Like gamblers, they all believe in themselves rather

What Not to Do

than in "luck." They believe they can control the odds because of their knowledge and strength of character. This risk-taking goes hand-in-hand with "impulsiveness" and "tough-mindedness"; they get their kicks from negotiating big deals which involve risk, which they hope will come out right in the end, but they know in their hearts that sometimes they must lose. And, often, because of the nature of the deal, the risk—and the rewards—can be enormous. If they lose, as they are bound to sometime, they lose everything. Once you are on the road, it is hard to stand back and really calculate the odds.

Many of the men who have lost everything must have known that the odds were against them. If they had seen anybody else doing what they themselves did, they would have been among the first to point out that it was financial suicide. But, having lost their objectivity, they still went forward because of the momentum of the deal or because their ego stopped them from being realistic. Since learning from others is the cornerstone of this book, let's look at some of those who had everything, but could not come to grips with the realities of the situation and took the chance that cost them everything—or sometimes just a bruised ego.

Jim Ling

Just a few years ago, Jim Ling was one of the most successful wheeler-dealers in America. He was everywhere. Hardly a day went by when you didn't read about Ling and his then fabulous L.T.V.—short for Ling-Temco-Vought.

In 1968, the year of the bull market, Ling was the chief executive officer, and major stockholder, of perhaps the hottest company on the New York Stock Exchange, at a time when the financial temperature generally was in the heat-wave zone. Ling and his company were almost in the big leagues—almost, but not quite—Ling himself hovering on the brink of shedding the somewhat double-edged label of wheeler-dealer and becoming part of the Establishment. The company was then only seven years old and, in those seven years, had risen to become one of the fifteen biggest companies in the United States. Its common stock was trading around $135 a share, and it was looking like an IBM or a Polaroid. Wall Street was dazzled. It seemed as though Ling was about to become a Wall Street legend in his own lifetime. He lived like a pasha in Dallas, had one of the biggest houses in that big-house town, had his own airline (Braniff), as well as a fleet of personal airplanes to take him and his executives to their various companies, and also a company ranch for rest and relaxation.

Ling was total energy. He looked, in the late 1960s, like a man who was ready to conquer the corporate world all by himself. *Signature* magazine once suggested that he had an "incurable overdose of adrenalin." Others have said that he was savagely competitive. He loved a proxy fight, or a takeover, purely for the thrill of the battle. He was the ultimate risk-taker. Life with no danger would be much too dull for Jim Ling. He made the game of business into something close to a body-contact sport. But he

What Not to Do

enjoyed his work too much, and, in the end, he took one risk too many. By the 1970s it looked as though it was all over for L.T.V. And he, himself, as one of the company's biggest stockholders, was one of the biggest losers. At the height, he was probably worth close to $100 million; at the end, no one knew what he was worth, but one thing is certain: Jim Ling's one mistake cost him a lot of money.

Jim Ling was the master of leverage. He would hock one company to buy another. He would spin off one subsidy to create a public market for its stock, so that he could borrow on its stock to buy another. He was interested in money—money to buy more and more companies. He wanted to acquire big, wealthy companies, most of them bigger at the time than L.T.V. itself. And he planned to buy them by either using his own company's stock as payment or by putting up that stock as collateral for loans. The stock, of course, was worth what the market said it was worth, and in those heady days of the 1960s the market said it was worth an awful lot of money. The higher the market price, the more valuable the stock, and the more money it provided for Ling to acquire yet more companies. His technique was really quite simple: The parts (the subsidiaries) are worth more than the whole (the parent) if the market says so. All you have to do is convince the market of the truth of that statement.

What usually happens when a company acquires other companies is that the parent company simply absorbs the acquired companies, along with the public stock. The market disappears, and the price of the company so acquired is theoretically reflected in the price of the parent company's stock. As each company is acquired, the original stockholders turn in their stock certificates, either for cash or a new certificate of the parent company. As a matter of market economics, the market value of the two companies, combined, is usually less than the market value of the two companies as independent entities. The reason for this is quite simple: The acquiring company has to pay with something, whether it's cash that it borrows or stock which it issues, thus reducing the value of the parent company by approximately the same amount as the price paid for the company acquired.

Ling's idea, like most great ideas, was simple. Reverse the process and make the market work *for* him, not against him. In 1965, he divided up L.T.V.'s principal operating divisions into three separate corporations: LTV Aerospace, LTV Electrosystems and LTV Ling-Altec. Each of the three then issued its own stock. The parent company kept roughly 75 to 80 percent of that stock in each case. The rest was offered to the public, who were the shareholders of L.T.V.

The public did what it was expected to do. Investors bid up and up, until the sum of the parts of the company was worth more than the whole. In terms of the market value, Jim Ling was now worth more than he had been when he owned one company, and more market value meant more money, which Ling could use to make more acquisitions. By shuffling paper, he had acquired something, in a sense, for nothing. Instead of the one stock certificate he had previously had to sell, use for borrowing or pledge, he now had four. So, not only did L.T.V.,

What Not to Do

with its 75 to 80 percent of each company, become richer, but Ling, as one of its major stockholders, became even richer, too.

All of this was risky business for any wheeler-dealer, and had Ling stopped here he still might be around today. But, like all gamblers, he could not resist just one more crack at the big one, so he used the stock of the subsidiary "public" companies to borrow $80 million to buy Wilson—a company that processed meat, made the famous Wilson sporting goods and owned Wilson Pharmaceuticals—and then did what nobody else would have the nerve to do. He moved the $80 million to Wilson's own books, split up the company into three parts and went public again. The money brought in by the public sale was enough to pay off almost all of the $80 million debt that he had transferred to Wilson's books. The stock of the three new companies went up again, and Jim Ling was a living legend. Not content with that, he then acquired Great America Corporation, which, in turn, owned Braniff Airlines and National Car Rental; and, as his finale, he went on to acquire the Jones and Laughlin Steel Company—what every wheeler-dealer doesn't need.

Then, in the market of 1969, it all came tumbling down. When the market fell, Ling didn't have to worry about one stock coming down—he had to worry about a dozen, and, as they say, what goes up in the market, also comes down. Leverage, as Ling should have remembered, works both ways—down, as well as up—and when it comes down, there is usually no one left to sell to and no one left to borrow from. Jim Ling learned, the hard way, the first rule of leverage: Bring it off and you are a star overnight; fail and you are out of the game forever.

Saul Steinberg

If risk is a key motivation for wheeling and dealing, then Saul Steinberg must be included among the risk-takers. Still active, still rich—though not quite so rich as he used to be—Steinberg made just one mistake, his attack on the Chemical Bank, but in a game like the deal game, where the stakes are high, one mistake was enough. He exemplifies to a "T" our definition of the man who forges ahead by the most extraordinary moves. He has ambition and guts and operates with flamboyance and supreme impatience. Is it any wonder that so many people regard him with disdain, jealousy and even contempt?

Born in Brooklyn, Saul started his company from scratch. In 1962, its net income was only $45,000—about what it might cost him now for alimony. He started by going public in 1965 with what was then a new idea, computer leasing. Today, thanks to the times and old-line Reliance Insurance Company of Philadelphia, he looks like he is there to stay. He reportedly once told a group of brokers, "I know you guys would like to get me out—but there is no way. I and my family own too much stock."

Steinberg's record was nearly perfect until February 1969. His stock was high and made good marks on Wall

What Not to Do

Street while his company was considered a growth company and all was go—especially after the brilliant takeover of Reliance Insurance Company of Philadelphia. But then came his assault on the United States' fifth largest bank, and since then Saul Steinberg has been very unhappy. Although he has made more money on his own than any other person his age, something seemed to have gone out of the man. He has certainly made money, won social recognition and had lots of fun, but has he satisfied his ego? The answer is probably no.

Going from success to success, and probably by this time beginning to believe his own press and publicity, Steinberg decided in February 1969 that what he really wanted to be was a banker. After all, Leasco was built on borrowed money, as are all leasing companies, and certainly bankers and banks were the chief items on each day's agenda of meetings. Through day-to-day contacts with bankers, Steinberg soon came to realize not only that these were the men with *real* power, because they were very much members of the Establishment, but also that they were not necessarily any smarter than he. So, he probably thought, "Hey, why not me?" But the prospect of being able to take over the Big One blinded Steinberg to many of the realities of the situation. No only did the bank beat him at his own game, but the attempt turned many of his business associates against him in a way he will probably never forget.

What Steinberg did shortly after he lost his Chemical battle best illustrates this point. He promptly bought, personally, the controlling interest in the Kings Lafayette Bank in Brooklyn. He was going to be a banker, and to hell with Chemical. He was elected chairman of the executive committee and started to reorganize the bank. At the first meeting, Steinberg suggested forming a holding company, which would be on the American Stock Exchange. The board readily agreed, the holding company was formed and they all sat back and waited for things to start happening. And then—nothing. The directors were lost; they didn't know what to do next. Apparently, nobody had considered how to go about getting enough money from the bank to the holding company without violating the banking law. It then transpired that Steinberg had had enough of banks and he wanted out. He sold his block of stock at a small loss and Kings Lafayette became part of the Republic National Bank of New York.

Glenn W. Turner

It is very hard for many people to distinguish between a promoter and a wheeler-dealer. Glenn W. Turner is included in this section not because he would qualify as a wheeler-dealer but because he was a promoter.

A promoter is, basically, a salesman who sells puff, not reality, and certainly not an idea or a concept that will last or has real substance. He tends to shock people with his methods; he is brash, aggressive and pushy. And, most of the time, his promotions will not stand the test of severe scrutiny. In the course of my own business experience I have found that if a promoter's deal is examined closely, using the principles set forth in this

What Not to Do

book, under its very attractive, seemingly straightforward exterior, it will usually be found to be unlawful or, if not that, then at least a little shady.

In the early 1970s, a client of mine was interested in going into the cosmetics business. It was, he said, the hottest franchise in the country—the Koscot line of cosmetics and beauty aids, run by a man named Glenn Turner. Would I look at it for him, he wanted to know, because he was thinking of investing about $5000. Well, look I did, and what I found was the old-fashioned pyramid promotion which has been used for years by promoters who are specialists in multilevel selling. In essence, the company starts out by selling distributorships —they can be for cosmetics, land in California's desert, pots and pans or just a self-improvement kit like a glorified Dale Carnegie course. The product must have one important feature—its cost must be low in relation to the selling price, so that the markup, from cost to retail, can accommodate a slice for each of an awful lot of middlemen. Now, the distributor gets a fairly large territory for his money, say it's the borough of Queens, which has a population as large as many of the small states in America. The distributor then sets up subdistributors, selling them a franchise for an amount which is usually half as much as he paid for the whole territory—and since he almost always sets up more than two subdistributors, he has already covered his initial outlay, without selling a single lipstick. The subdistributors set up sales managers, or wholesalers, who again pay the subdistributors for the privilege of operating in the territory, and then the sales manager sells smaller territories to the people who are supposed to do the actual selling—either part-time women or men who are looking for a second job—and so on, almost ad infinitum.

On the surface, it looks like the Avon Products operation, or the Fuller Brush operation, or the Tupperware operation, but it's not like them at all in its business purpose. In those companies, what is actually being sold is the product. In a typical pyramid operation, the sale is in the distributorships, and the product is merely window dressing. Each man in the pyramid, like in a chain letter, makes his profit by convincing someone else to sell a subdistributorship, *not* from selling the actual product. In fact, the product has so little to do with the promotion that it would make no difference at all whether it was skin cream or pots and pans. In order for a program like this to succeed, it must be initiated and sold by a great salesman—for salesmanship is what it's all about—and there is no doubt that Glenn Turner is a great salesman. The meetings at which he spoke have been described as a cross between an Elmer Gantry revivalist meeting and an early Beatles' concert at Shea Stadium. The mind just reels to think what he might have achieved if only he'd had something to sell.

The New York Attorney General's office, in investigating the Turner Koscot operation, took special note of the fact that Turner's representatives were painting pie-in-the-sky pictures at sales meetings, waving fat checks around and suggesting that Koscot distributors could make $50,000 to $100,000 a year by selling to their sub-

What Not to Do

distributors. It calculated that at the end of 1970 there were 1600 distributors in Turner's state alone, and, at $5000 each, that's one large amount of money earned by him and his friends in exchange for an idea and nothing else. It was calculated that were the 1600 distributors in that state alone to make $100,000 each by bringing in other subdistributors, they would have to recruit 150,000 more subdistributors into Koscot within one year, and these would have to add another 150 million by the end of the second year. You don't need a mathematical genius to see that if all these subsubsubdistributors sold just one bottle of tanning lotion, there would be enough of the stuff to irrigate the Sahara desert.

The whole deal was so obviously a promotion, and not a business proposition, that it is amazing that so many people fell for it. "The scope of the fraud and misrepresentations and the amount of money being exacted from unsuspecting citizens . . . is enormous," said the Pennsylvania Attorney General in his court proceeding against Koscot. "The social implications are equally enormous when one considers that most of these people who invest in this program will be innocent lambs being led to slaughter by a dream of 'heaven on earth.' Most of these people will go into debt or will convert their life savings, and at least three out of four will be doomed to failure."

Of course, the whole thing collapsed because it was never meant to be a real cosmetics business but rather just one big chain letter, just one gigantic promotion.

MONEY, EGO, POWER

Keith Barrish

Keith Barrish, and his Gramco, were not as well known in America as his big-name competitor, Bernie Cornfeld, but, for a while, he looked just as successful. Barrish and Cornfeld had a lot in common. They both ran offshore funds domiciled and headquartered in Panama, Luxembourg or the Bahamas. They both sold their funds to foreign investors, thus avoiding the scrutiny of the Securities and Exchange Commission in America. They both hired as highly visible directors people with famous names to give their funds instant respectability. Keith Barrish had no less than Pierre Salinger, President Kennedy's former press aide; the ex-mayor of New York, Robert Wagner; the ex-governor of California, "Pat" Brown; and other international politicians. But Gramco went one better on Cornfeld's new approach—it sold real estate, the so-called safest investment in the world, rather than stocks on the United States stock exchanges.

In order to understand Gramco fully, you must understand the nature of mutual funds and the difference between the "closed-end" funds and the "open-end" funds. Bernie Cornfeld's fund, like the American open-end funds, were subject to redemption at any time by the subscribers. That's why Cornfeld invested in stocks which could always be sold on the various United States stock exchanges and provide him with the liquidity he needed. Barrish's fund, USIF, was also open-ended, but, here, the investments were not stocks with a market but first-class real estate properties. For years, everyone thought real estate was better than stocks as an invest-

What Not to Do

ment—safer certainly—and Keith Barrish was out to prove it. Gramco operated on the premise that the American economy was caught in an unending inflationary spiral and that real estate values had nowhere to go but up. By buying shares of USIF, a subsidiary of Gramco, you put your money into real estate rather than into common stocks. So far, so good. But, the old rule in real estate is that in bad times there are no buyers. This may also be true for stocks, but you can usually find a buyer if you are prepared to make your price low enough. That is why the United States Securities and Exchange Commission has not allowed a fund to invest in real estate if it wants to be open ended and subject to redemptions. The closed-end funds are nothing more than glorified corporations whose purpose is investment rather than operation as a business. The Securities and Exchange Commission takes the position that it's dangerous for a fund to be in assets like real estate if there is a run on the fund, since it may not be possible to achieve the liquidity you need if the market is down. But Barrish, by operating offshore, didn't have to worry about the Securities and Exchange Commission interfering.

At first, things went well. The fund operated out of the Bahamas and the sales were made only to foreigners. In three years, the fund attracted 23,000 shareholders in Europe, Latin America and the Far East. The overwhelming majority of the investors were small, owning about $12,000 each. According to the company's rosy sales talk, the value of the shares would increase as the property became more valuable, but, of course, with real estate, nobody really knows what the property is worth until it is sold. That, as it turned out, was only one small problem for the shareholders of USIF. The big problem for Keith Barrish's thousands of stockholders began when some of them wanted to redeem their shares for cash. As long as they were few, Barrish could cope, but as the numbers increased, so did Barrish's problems. That old legendary problem came to the fore—how do you sell the property to pay back investors?

It seems that the old rules still held, and one morning Barrish woke up and found himself suffering from a massive run on his cash reserves. Tight money, a bad stock market and Bernie Cornfeld's problems all led to a loss of confidence, and the one thing that Barrish believed would never happen happened: Everyone wanted his money back at once, and Gramco and Barrish were finished.

7

A Four-Point Game Plan

By this time you should have a grasp of the essentials of wheeling and dealing and should be ready to get your first game plan down on paper. Writing things down is always a good idea, since it helps you to clarify your own ideas, and whomever you go to for help, whether it is a banker, broker, lawyer, accountant or friend, will want to see a proposal of what you intend to do.

The Idea

First of all, there are certain questions you must ask yourself—for instance, *what is my basic idea or concept?*

Remember that times are changing and investors now are more discerning, making it all the more important that your ideas be new and exciting. The namesake and descendant of the famous British painter Joshua Reynolds, a thirty-three-year-old dropout from the brokerage firm of Hayden Stone, had just an idea—"mood" rings. After tension forced him out of Wall Street, in 1972, Reynolds launched Q-Tran (for "Tranquillity") with the intention of running a meditation center for the chronically nervous. But then he got the idea for a "feedback" ring. The ring would contain a stone which had been chemically treated so that it changes color as your body heat—and, therefore, your emotional temperature—rises and falls. When you are tranquil, the ring is a cool turquoise, but when you are intensely happy, it assumes a hot, purple color. There is no magic involved; the stone is simply heat-sensitive. If you put it in the icebox, it turns black, while on a hot stove it would become blue. And the formula for such a chemically treated stone has been around for years—used widely in hospitals to detect fever, on electrical circuits and even in three-dimensional movie spectacles—but what got the idea off the ground in such a big way in 1975 was Reynolds' promotional flair. He took on partners, like the press agent who was also handling the Fabergé cosmetic account and who received 1 percent of the action, who could help promote the ring and market it as "The Christmas Gift of the Year."

Soon Polly Bergen, then president of a Fabergé subsidiary bearing her name, became a large stockholder, and Eugenia Sheppard, the Publishers-Hall Syndicate columnist, wrote an article on the ring and Joshua Reynolds. The newspapers in New York and Los Angeles picked up the story, as did *People* magazine, and before you knew it, Bonwit Teller was selling the rings at forty-

A Four-Point Game Plan

five dollars each, as fast as Reynolds could deliver them. Paul Newman owns one, and so do Barbra Streisand, Dustin Hoffman, Margaux Hemingway and the Steve McQueens. It was the hottest novelty since Art Linkletter's Hula-Hoop.

All this publicity has turned Reynolds into a famous man but, alas, not a rich one. In order to get the idea off the ground, it seems that Reynolds was forced to sell all but 10 percent of Q-Tran to keep afloat. And, in spite of his brokerage background, he was totally unprepared for the phenomenal success of his product. Because he was unable to manufacture and supply the rings to keep up with the demand, his chance of making it big in the deal business, first time out, was destroyed. Had Reynolds been better prepared for his venture, had he established sufficient banking credit and organization—in other words, had he read this book—he would by now have been very rich.

Raising the Necessary Funds

There is simply no way of moving your idea forward until you have this phase of the operation well in hand. The dangers of moving without adequate finance are legion; witness the downfall of A. S. Beck.

The A. S. Beck Shoe Company, with its chain of women's shoe stores, was one of those companies which had never made any real money, but had never lost enough to be in serious financial trouble. There were many factors to make it an attractive proposition for a wheeler-dealer. For one thing, it was already listed on the American Stock Exchange, so that its stock could be more readily used in an acquisition than the stock of a company the same size which was being traded over the counter. For another, its credit standing with suppliers, its bank connections through years of being in the same business, and its assets, gave it a certain financial strength. The only problem with Beck, the reason it hadn't been snapped up before by a high-flying conglomerateur, was that the shoe business wasn't profitable and the company was too heavily committed to it, by virtue of the long leases on its retail stores, to change direction.

In 1969, along came Newton Gleckel, lately of Divco-Wayne, and then of the *New York Daily Column,* bringing with him Chuck McDevitt, who himself had acquired something of a reputation in the deal business during his time with Boise Cascade. It was Gleckel, however, who bought the necessary stock to take control of the company, by means of deferred payments. (This information, usually so closely guarded by the people involved, came to light as the result of lawsuits brought in 1971.) Initially, he bought all the stock in the hands of the previous owners, partly with cash, partly with borrowed money, and agreed to buy the rest of the stock at higher prices at a later date. This is a very neat trick if you can pull it off because, for a minimum outlay of cash, it provides you with the maximum amount of leverage.

Let's assume that you need to buy 500,000 shares at $8 a share to gain control of the company. You could purchase all the stock outright, which would cost you

A Four-Point Game Plan

$4 million. If you were able to raise an 80 percent loan against the stock, you would still have to find $800,000 yourself—a sizable outlay on one deal.

If, on the other hand, you bought the stock on a deferred payment plan, buying 100,000 shares at $8 a share the first year, another 100,000 the following year at $9, 200,000 the year after at $10, and the remaining 100,000 the next year at $12, all you would need initially (assuming that you managed to get an 80 percent loan) is $160,000—a much more manageable sum.

Suppose at the end of the following year, when you are due to pay for another 100,000 shares at $9 each, the actual market value of the shares is $12. You are buying $1.2 million worth of stock for $900,000—an instant profit, on paper, of $300,000, enough to cover the interest on the loans you already have and to persuade the bank to grant you a further loan for this payment, so that you don't need to find any new cash for your second installment. As long as the value of the stock is rising, you can complete the whole deal this way, using the profits from your equity to pay not only for the interest on the loans, but for the stock itself.

Having gained control of Beck that way, Gleckel left the day-to-day running of the company to McDevitt, who began to do as he had done at Boise Cascade, and make acquisitions. In two years, Beck acquired twenty-nine companies—over a company a month. Although McDevitt had done well at Boise, he had neither the experience nor the reputation of Newton Gleckel, so it was Gleckel who had persuaded the banks to loan them money, some

$20 million in all, to pay for all these acquisitions—many of which were bought on deferred payment plans, naturally.

But then, trouble. In 1970, the market took a downward turn, and the stock they were committed to buy at fixed prices was not even reaching that price on the open market, let alone making the profit Gleckel was depending on to pay off the interest on the money he had borrowed. Money in general became tight. The banks would not loan Gleckel the money he needed to pay for the companies McDevitt had acquired, and, financial wheeling and dealing aside, they had not even begun to solve the problems they had originally inherited with A. S. Beck. The result was that in 1970 McDevitt and Gleckel both resigned, even though it seems likely that the company could have been saved if the right man had been appointed originally.

The story of Gleckel and his time at Beck is a cautionary tale from which several important lessons are to be learned. For a start, always use as little cash to get into a company as you can, *but* make sure that you have the backing of a bank or at least of wealthy partners to guarantee your loans. You must realize, too, that leverage works two ways. If you pull it off, you'll be a very rich man; if you don't, then you're out of the game permanently. Be positive and optimistic, but don't be ostrich-like about possible disaster. You must have well-thought-out contingency plans in case the market takes a downward turn, or money gets tight or the acquisitions don't pan out.

A Four-Point Game Plan

The Use of the Money

Once you have arranged the necessary financing, make sure you know exactly how you are going to use it and what percentage of the money will be used for each part of the operation. It is best to outline your concept, allocating the amount of funds necessary for each phase of the concept. Joshua Reynolds, for example, should have at least set aside a sum for the manufacturing of the samples, the necessary models, the manufacturing facilities—either his own or those of a subcontractor—the filing of a patent, the packaging, advertising and public relations, the cost of billing and collection of the accounts receivable. Obviously, you'll never have all the funds you need in hand if the concept is more successful than you anticipate, but at least you can set down on paper the order of priorities for the use of your financing. Consider the repayment of loans to friends and banks, and make provisions in advance for their repayment from sales or from additional sources. Of course, having your own funds makes all the difference in the world.

Look at how Julio Tanjeloff has parlayed the success of his Astro Mineral Gallery of Gems in New York into a retail empire. A lawyer by profession, Tanjeloff had been involved in mining, metals, real estate and ranching in Argentina before coming to the United States in 1961. Two years later, with his own money, he opened his first Astro Mineral Gallery in New York. As in Reynolds' case, the concept was simple. Jewelry made of precious stones was becoming so absurdly expensive that Tanjeloff decided to introduce jewelry of nonprecious stones. The idea was not a new one. But Tanjeloff took it a stage further by selling not only jewelry, but also the minerals in their natural uncut state as collector's items, decorations for the home and gifts.

The idea was an instant success, and, having added to the galleries a mineral collectors' magazine, an advertising agency and several other businesses, Tanjeloff had created a base from which he was able to acquire a whole group of old-established New York retailers with first-class reputations who had fallen on hard times. He bought Georg Jensen from a syndicate put together by Bill Bernbach of the Doyle Dane Bernbach agency, and the Kenton Collection from the Kenton Corporation, one of Meshulam Riklis's rare retailing mistakes. The price for the latter was low—$305,000 in cash and $10.4 million of Kenton's debts—which illustrates the classic rule of wheeling and dealing: use as little cash as possible and assume as much of the debt which the company you are acquiring has outstanding so that the need for new financing is limited. The easiest way to buy a company is either with its own money or with existing debt. Witness Grassie and Beck. Banks and other creditors almost always prefer to extend an existing loan to the new operator rather than liquidate the company to recover the debt. It's a face-saving device for the creditors, and there is always, potentially, a bonus for the banks in the shape of a good new customer. In this case, no doubt the banks and insurance companies who were owed money by Jensen and Kenton were delighted to have a man of Tan-

A Four-Point Game Plan

jeloff's proven ability take over the two struggling enterprises.

In addition, Tanjeloff has picked up the lease on the S. Klein store on Union Square in New York City and the Rosenthal Studio-Haus chain of giftware shops which has a store on Fifth Avenue and several other prestige premises. It's true that his buys have all been faltering retail operations, but Tanjeloff believes that he can make them pay with his new concept of importing large volumes of merchandise from European manufacturers at a lower cost than anyone else. In each instance, Tanjeloff, who is known in the trade as a one-man band, used his own money to make these deals and intends to use his own capital to revive all of the stores as places where middle-income and upper-income people can find bargains, and where he can become richer still.

The Capital Structure

All of these concepts need a base upon which to operate the capital structure that will spell success. The kind of organization to be used and the rights and obligations of each of the participants should be spelled out in great detail from the very beginning. First, understand that the capital on which you must operate is the property or money actually received by the company in return for the stock that it issues, based on "par value" (actual value) or on an arbitrarily decided "no par-value." Second, the shares of capital stock actually represent the interest that the holder has in the company, his percentage of the equity or his piece of the action. To do all the work, as Joshua Reynolds did, and be left with a mere 10 percent of the action is not what wheeling and dealing is all about.

It might not be possible to buy as much equity in the company as you would like at the beginning, but when stock prices of public companies start failing, as they are bound to do every few years, then you can buy back your own stock at the market's bargain-basement prices and increase your equity by going private again. Don't expect such a move to win you many friends among the stockholders who bought your stock when prices were high and who are now being forced to sell it back to you at a much lower price.

Examine the case of Mary Wells Lawrence, cited earlier, or of Booz, Allen and Hamilton, the internationally renowned business consultants who went public at $24 a share in 1970 and recently announced plans to buy back their stock from the public at a mere $7.75 a share and go private. This is a great way to make a lot of money and increase your stake in your company's equity.

8

Where Do You Go from Here?

You have arrived. You are chairman of the board and the chief executive officer. You have acquired some equity in the company. Now is the time to assess your position very carefully and decide where you go from here.

Before you make any decisions about the future, take a close look at the company you now control. Now that you have reached the position to which you have aspired for years, your future depends entirely upon the kind of success you make of the company, and that, in turn, depends very largely on the kind of company you have taken over. Ask yourself what kind of business you are *really* in, and is it a good business to be in at this particular time? Does the company have enough capital and resources to enable you to expand when the opportunity arises, or is it in such poor shape financially that your options are hopelessly limited from the start?

If the company operates in the field of science or technology or some other specialist area beyond the scope of your personal knowledge, then call in independent experts to evaluate the situation for you. If the answers with which they present you suggest that the company is on the road to disaster, then change its direction, if possible, as soon as you can. If their answers indicate that the company is sound, then find ways of making it even more successful.

If your company is going to be a profit-making concern, then it is essential not only to have the right product or service but also to be able to sell it at a profit. Be sure you understand your margins—the difference between what it costs you, overall, to produce the item and its selling price. The selling price is determined not only by your costs and profit but also by what the market will stand and the price at which your competitors are selling their product. If an item costs you $9.50 to produce, even if you add on only 50 cents' profit and sell it at $10, you are not going to sell very many if your competitors are offering the item at $9.

Weigh the merits of your product very carefully. Ask yourself why a customer would buy yours and not your competitor's. Is yours better-made or does it have some unique feature? Is there a real demand for the product in the first place, and if so, what is it?

If your product is not so very different from everyone else's, why not consider a new marketing method to make it unique? Look at Estée Lauder. She introduced her cosmetics in department and specialty stores only, while her competitors, including her great rival, Revlon, sold their products in drugstores and even supermar-

Where Do You Go from Here?

kets. It meant that she wasn't doing the volume of business that they were doing, but it gave her products "class," one of the most important factors in the company's success.

As the new management of an old company, you must evaluate very fully what went wrong in the past. It could be fatal simply to dismiss the company's previous problems as the result of poor management. Find out why it could not keep its head above water or why, given that it has a great product, its success was so limited. Perhaps the product, good though it was, met every criterion except one. Take the Permamatic camera. It was an excellent product, superbly made, but it was too expensive to produce. The lowest price at which it could be sold, if the manufacturers were to make even a small profit, was fifty dollars, and the demand for cameras in that price range was very limited. Or, look at magazines. You could be producing a first-class editorial product, but if people are not buying it, then the advertisers will not buy the space between those superb photographs and splendid articles, and the magazine will not make money. *Penthouse* magazine, on the other hand, is a rather inferior copy of *Playboy* in its editorial content, and, yet, because it has a ready, interested market, it attracts all the advertising it needs and makes money.

Most businessmen, at some time in their careers, dream of finding a product that will revolutionize technology—another Xerox or Polaroid—and some spend millions of dollars, years of work and the talents of some first-class brains on research and development, pursuing that dream. But all too often the result is a product that

Money, Ego, Power

does not work or, worse, does not sell, and the company goes down trying. Never indulge a dream too long, or spend too much money in pursuing it at the expense of your tried and tested bread-and-butter products. That smacks of an idealism that you simply cannot afford if you are to survive in big business. You must be practical and make what you know will sell. By all means, experiment; if you don't, how can your company develop? But maintain a sense of proportion in your spending so that the company stays on an even keel and generates enough profit to subsidize future research and to keep your stockholders happy. Your success or failure as chairman will be judged largely in terms of the company's profits, and if there are no profits, then all the advances you have made in other areas will count for very little. Without company profits, you are just another businessman. With them, you are a successful businessman.

9

Life Style

The life style that usually accompanies the position of chairman in a company is a double-edged sword. It is one of the more succulent carrots dangled in front of you on your not necessarily long, though always hard, climb to the top; it is also part of the satin-lined trap which will keep you working just as hard once you've reached the top, to make sure that you stay there.

The Best of Everything

As the chairman, you can expect the best of everything: the biggest, most luxuriously appointed office, the most efficient secretary, a private company car plus chauffeur, first-class travel either in the company's private plane or on scheduled airlines, the best suites at the best hotels —in fact, every conceivable luxury that can pass the scrutiny of the Internal Revenue Service in the United States as a write-off against tax.

The rationale behind it is simple. You work hard for the company, and it rewards you, not only with a generous salary and perhaps stock options, too, but also with the perks, as they call them in the United Kingdom, or the fringe benefits as they say in the United States, which allow you to have a $100,000 life style on a $50,000 salary. It suits the company to play it that way because it is easier to justify expenses than higher salaries, which have to be declared to the stockholders in the company's annual report. If your company is grossing $10 million a year, the $100,000 your fringe benefits are costing is a mere 1 percent of the gross—a figure that will go virtually unnoticed.

It is also to your personal advantage to play it big that way. A modest salary and plenty of perks make better fiscal sense than drawing a huge salary and paying for the extras yourself. If you are earning $100,000 a year, you are in the 50 percent bracket. You don't need to be a financial genius to realize that you obviously can't afford a car and chauffeur at $20,000 a year. Much better to earn, say, $50,000, pay less tax and have the car on the company, since the government will meet about half the cost, anyway, through company tax allowances. But your trips in the company car—whoever is actually footing the bill—will almost certainly be just a small part of the traveling you'll be doing on company business in the United States and all over the world. Since time is money, naturally, for the most part you will fly.

Most big companies these days have their own plane.

Life Style

Some giants like AT&T, Eastman Kodak and American Can have entire fleets of corporate aircraft, and special departments within the organization to handle operations. Key executives of these corporations are cushioned in luxury on their business trips, courtesy of the government since the corporate tax structure allows each flight to be written off against tax. In theory, company airplanes are strictly for business trips, which perhaps explains why the billion dollars' worth of corporate aircraft parked on the tarmac at Miami a few years back during the Superbowl football game had their registration numbers carefully blacked out. They would have made extremely interesting reading, not only for the Treasury Department but also for any zealous stockholders with an eye on diminishing company profits.

Most corporations these days have at least one company plane, and, depending upon the company's gross sales though certainly not its profits, it might be anything from a Queen or King Air propjet that costs anywhere from $250,000 to $600,000 to a Lear 24 or 25 that would cost from $800,000 to $1.5 million. For the larger corporations, fan-jet Falcons start at around $1.5 million and sell pretty briskly, while for the really big spenders, like Eugene Klein, the ultimate ego trip is the Grumman Gulfstream II, the king of the corporate jets, which would set you back $3.5 to $4 million before you even got it off the ground.

It makes financial sense for a Detroit-based company like Chrysler to maintain an apartment in the Waldorf Towers in New York or apartments in London to accommodate their chief executives on their frequent trips to

Money, Ego, Power

New York and London. It did not make sense for Curtis Publishing to maintain an apartment at the Carlton House in New York City during the mid-1960s; it was used only rarely, and, though the company at that stage could ill afford it, was kept to impress the occasional visitor.

It would be a very blasé visitor who failed to be impressed by the Greenbrier suite, a triplex in Cleveland's Terminal Tower used by the Chessie System for entertaining visiting businessmen and for the occasional conference. Decorated in his usual lavish style by Carleton Varney, it is impressive enough to have been featured in some of the top interior design magazines and, no doubt, to have boosted the egos of many tired businessmen. Corporate apartments have caught on in such a big way that a large recently completed cooperative apartment and office building complex called the Olympic Tower on Fifth Avenue and Fifty-first Street is offering its apartments at six figures apiece.

But not all company residences are lavish city apartments; there was Jimmy Ling's Texas ranch, where many a banker learned to enjoy a good old-fashioned Texas barbecue. If your own company or the company with which you are doing business has not yet gotten onto the corporate-apartment scene, then you will have to rough it in a suite at a top hotel. Since you are living on an expense account, you will naturally eat at the best restaurants, where around forty dollars a head is about par for the course (or courses), and go to the most exclusive nightclubs or, if your brow is a little higher, the latest smash-hit play without even blinking at the scalper's

Life Style

rates you are charged for the tickets. And if your company is liberal-minded and the accountant sufficiently creative in his tax returns, you can also enjoy the most attractive female company without it costing you, personally, a penny. Don't be misled into believing that your company's motives are purely altruistic. Getting you accustomed to the good life which you could not hope to afford on your salary is one sure way of making certain that you not only want to stay in your job but also that you work hard to ensure that you do. Once you have a taste for the Beverly Hills Hotel and the Bistro, you'll find it very hard to settle for the Holiday Inn and the House of Pies, so even if you do become dissatisfied with your job, you are more than likely to count your blessings and your reimbursable expenses and sit tight!

And, of course, unless you have a uniquely strong character, you will want to carry your expense-account life style through into your private life as well. Naturally, you want your home to reflect your status, but a tiny cooperative apartment in New York (with a not-so-tiny ever-increasing maintenance charge) will cost you at least $100,000 while the Beverly Hills mansion with swimming pool and tennis court will set you back at least $500,000. Of course, everybody knows what it costs to live in London, Paris or Geneva today. Then, it is unlikely that you will want to furnish your home from the Sears Roebuck catalogue. FFF (fine French furniture to the uninitiated) is what you should aim for, or fine English—preferably eighteenth-century—or early American now that it is becoming fashionable, and, of course, any suitable pieces from the modern "name" designers.

While you are filling your house with superb furniture, you can hardly cover your walls with anything less than originals by a few well-known artists. Eugene Klein, for instance, went for Modigliani and Picasso. Paying $500,000 for a painting may give you pause, but you should not look at it simply as something to hang on your wall. Think of it as an investment. If you have taken the time and trouble to find out about art, it could be an investment that will pay you handsome dividends in the long run, and, in the short run, it will give you a lot more visual pleasure than a deposit box full of stocks and bonds.

Naturally, you will require help to run the house. A couple—housekeeper-cook, butler-gardener-general handyman—will cost you around $1500 a month, assuming of course that the accommodations you are offering come up to their very high standards. If you have very young children, a baby nurse will cost you at least another $125 a week. A chauffeur, at around $125 a week, will probably be on the company's books, not yours, as a legitimate business expense. Although, with luck, your couple should be perfectly satisfactory for your day-to-day requirements, you will need a gourmet chef to cook for your dinner parties once or twice a month, and he will charge you around twenty dollars a head, excluding wine and the cost of the extra serving staff.

Eventually, all of this lavish living, and having to work so hard to pay for it all, will begin to take its toll on your nerves, so you will then start looking for a country or beach house where you can relax on those all-too-short weekends. And don't think that just because it is a second

Life Style

home that you can furnish it with cast-offs—it must reflect your growing good taste. Since relaxing does not mean simply dozing in a chair—much as you might wish it did—you may also need a boat, or a swimming pool, or tennis court, or even a small golf-driving range.

While you are enjoying your possessions, you must look the part, too. Mass-produced, off-the-rack suits are out. Yours must be custom-made in the finest tweeds and wools. If you really are taking success seriously, you will fly to London and leave your measurements on file with Thomas Nutter or Rupert Lycett-Green of Blades for your suits and coats, and with Turnbull and Asser for shirts. You can also have your own last made at Lobb, the bootmaker in St. James, but unless you need riding boots or like old-fashioned shoes, you'll probably pick up several pairs of loafers at Gucci in Paris, Rome or Florence.

Your wife, naturally, will not want to appear dowdy in comparison with you, so you will have to get accustomed to paying bills from European couturiers, furriers and jewelers. Your children, once they get tired of T-shirts, jeans and sneakers, will start to develop expensive tastes, too.

Running a corporation and maintaining a high-powered life style is a taxing business, and, therefore, you will need intermittent vacations to recharge your batteries. Each year, the quest for relaxation will take you farther and farther afield to the season's newest exotic paradise, not yet on the tourist routes and known only to jet-setters and other wheeler-dealers. In the early 1970s it was the Costa Smeralda, then Seychelles and Bali. This year, who knows?

The aim, of course, is to get away from most of it—but by no means all. Use your vacation to make new social contacts, to develop your taste for fine wine and exotic food, and for local art and architecture. Many a vacationer has come home from distant parts with a bug—not just the usual dysentery but the collecting bug. Collecting does not automatically mean paintings and sculpture; it could be anything from antique cars or airplanes to islands in the sun or oases in the desert. And, as with paintings and sculpture, a new hobby can become another area in which to wheel and deal that can boost your bank balance as well as your ego.

All of these pleasures, though, have to be paid for out of your own pocket, and it is extremely unlikely that your pocket will ever hold enough to cover the cost of your life style. So your personal line of credit at the bank will be stretched taut, and the collateral you put up for your loans—houses, paintings, jewelry—will probably be the very items that got you into hock in the first place. It is a very obvious trap, but such a comfortable one that people like you are leaping into it, eyes wide open, all the time.

Advice to the Wife

If you're the wife of a would-be wheeler-dealer and you're interested in remaining one of his most valuable assets both on the way to and at the top, you'd best begin your own training program immediately in order to keep up with him—or to lead the way. Don't make the mis-

Life Style

takes that many other wives, now ex-wives, have made in the past. Don't neglect your own growth and development and be content simply to bask in your husband's reflected glory, because you may well find that when he reaches the top, you will be spun off in favor of a new, more attractive acquisition whose physical attractiveness is only one of her many advantages.

Remember that while your husband is out setting the business world on fire, he will be meeting many intelligent, capable, attractive women who not only hold down very well-paid and responsible jobs, but who also manage their own lives, marriages and families with the same efficiency and grace. If you limit your horizons to shopping, going to the hairdresser's and washing diapers, and your conversation to what the kids did today and what the woman in the supermarket said about your neighbors, your husband won't fail to notice the contrast and you can't help but suffer by comparison.

Limiting your scope to home and family is dangerous. Once your wheeling-dealing husband earns enough money, hire efficient household help and use your newly acquired spare time for self-enrichment. You might take some art courses and prepare yourself in advance for the days when your husband becomes a so-called "collector," a hobby characteristic of most wheeler-dealers. Then, one day you might find him turning to you for advice. Make yourself the kind of person he loves to have around—an intelligent, attractive woman, a gracious hostess, loyal helpmate, an independent person with enough personal resources to sustain you during the long hours when he is away.

Money, Ego, Power

All this time on your own might provide just the impetus to return to the work you did before you were married or to try your hand at some new interest. It is not just a question of earning money; it is important for you —and for him—to know that you are capable of holding a job in your own right, doing something creative and feeling the sense of accomplishment that comes from doing a good job.

If you're not working, or if your work is portable, go with him on his business trips. Traveling with your husband can be fun. You can fill your days with sightseeing, trips to museums or looking up old acquaintances, and he will appreciate having someone to come home to at the end of a long, hard day. Or perhaps there is a way you can involve yourself in his work. The time you spend away is a fine opportunity to grow closer together, and it is much better than sitting at home, feeling lonely and hating him for leaving you.

Your main objective should be to keep up with him. It isn't necessary to compete, but you should be developing, growing, expanding and exploring at the same time that he is. Moving forward together is much more fun than going it alone. And if you don't believe it, ask some of the first wives of wheeler-dealers who are sitting at home today bitterly reading about their ex-husbands in the business pages and ruing the day that they gave up on life. Many of them claim: "Success spoiled the man." This provides a handy excuse, but a more careful study of the relationships existing prior to the wheeler-dealer stage of these couples' lives often proves far more illuminating in tracing the reasons for a divorce. Many

Life Style

wheeler-dealers marry young. Compound all the problems usually inherent in early marriages between two relatively immature and inexperienced people, add the mate's compelling drive for success, and you have a sure-fire recipe for a problematic future.

Divorce, in general, is on the increase—the latest figures suggest that almost one in two marriages ends in divorce. It may seem that the divorce rate is higher among successful people, but remember that theirs are the divorces reported most often by the papers and that only the very rich can afford to support two families these days. Regardless of who precipitates the divorce, it is always an unpleasant experience in personal terms; practically speaking, though, it is just one more business deal, albeit a very expensive one, to be worked out with the attorneys and accountants.

Sex

Another factor to be considered in the wheeler-dealer divorce pattern is sex. For most wheeler-dealers, there are two kinds of sex—marital and extramarital.

MARITAL SEX

There appears to be a direct correlation between the Dow Jones average and a wheeler-dealer's sexual activity. When the thirty leading industrials are bullish, so is the wheeler-dealer. When business is good, he is feeling good, his mind and body are stimulated, problems seem less significant and his expectations are high. On the increase, too, are his sexual appetites. Conversely, a bearish market makes for a bearish sex life, with appetites and desires sharply diminished. Obviously, the mind—and the market—play an important role in sexual desire.

The years 1969 through 1975 were bad economically. Wall Street was suffering, and so were the sex lives of the business moguls. With the added strain of the poor economy, it wasn't surprising that many marriages, already under stress, culminated in divorces during this period. Considering the dismal economic climate of the mid-1970s, the divorce statistics should make interesting reading.

EXTRACURRICULAR SEX

To most men who travel on a regular basis, sex on the road constitutes a popular pastime. Guilt feelings are allayed by the sheer distance between the adulterer and spouse. And the fact that he will never again see this particular woman dispels the husband's fear of being found out.

Girls are often provided by the local company office as a means of rounding out the day's activities. On the higher levels the businessman himself never has to pass money to the girl—that's done by the local procurer—so the poor chap can delude himself into thinking that it is his pot belly and bald head that have attracted the atten-

Life Style

tions of the lovely young thing who arrives on his doorstep. For the girls, it is strictly business and (considering how long they usually spend with the client) they are about as well paid for their time as the business moguls are for their services.

Historically, the movie industry has always attracted a surfeit of attractive, ambitious girls, and the West Coast is certainly one of the business trips favored by most eastern, midwestern and European executives—as is Paris. Beverly Hills and Paris provide idyllic playgrounds with many good-looking girls who have yet to find an easier way to make a living. Men who have been going to the West Coast or to Paris on a regular basis usually have their own list of established contacts—perhaps girls they used to see who now furnish them with new recommendations. Many wheeler-dealers who commute regularly keep a special girl in pin money—or maintain her exclusively—to ensure their priority. And if things get slow in Los Angeles or Paris, Las Vegas and the Riviera are only a short trip away.

Cost varies according to geography and quality, and prices soar when a man's ego comes into play. If a girl who normally charges a hundred dollars knows that her client thinks of himself as a real big-time wheeler-dealer, she may well ask for three hundred, which makes them both happy. She is delighted with the extra money, and he is delighted with the resulting ego boost. Some men feel better paying a thousand dollars for a girl. Paying over the odds entitles them to a free reign, so that a hundred-dollar girl could prove to be a thousand-dollar experience. Most wheeler-dealers prefer to get their extracurricular sex for money rather than love, because having an affair, getting involved with just one girl, can be very dangerous. Regular contact inevitably leads to a relationship, and if that relationship develops and deepens, then the man's marriage is threatened. Others have wives who permit them to come and go as they please, as long as they continue to support them in grand style and avoid embarrassing them. For such men, marriage serves as a kind of insurance policy. The excuse of a wife and family is the best defense against any burning discussions about the future of a relationship or any change in what may be a very satisfactory status quo.

The man who has an affair is putting his marriage to the ultimate test, and chances are that there is already a problem with his marriage. Therefore, it's not surprising that many such situations end in divorce. He may not always marry the particular girl he had the affair with, but she has given him the impetus to get out while providing the love and affection he needed to sustain him during the breakup of his marriage.

If he does marry again, the likelihood of the second marriage surviving is quite good. If nothing else both he and his Mark II wife know what he does not want from a partner, and also second marriages are usually undertaken with a great deal more forethought. Having been disappointed in himself for his first failure, feeling guilty for disrupting the lives of his children and feeling pinched for the money that his first wife has demanded, the wheeler-dealer goes into a second union with a cooler eye and a much more practical outlook. Furthermore, the man who has been through a divorce and a

Life Style

remarriage knows that the anticipation of a divorce is much worse than the actuality, and he wouldn't hesitate to do it again—and do it quickly—if necessary.

SEX IN THE OFFICE

During the course of every working day, a large number of women in offices are faced with the decision of whether or not to sleep with the boss, or one of those men close to the boss. Sometimes, it begins with a casting-couch scene to get a job, and later on it might seem the best way to get a promotion. For a few, it could be just a strong attraction, with a bit of infatuation and even love mixed in.

Office romances are not confined to the single or divorced woman. Married women are just as often approached, and sometimes they do the approaching themselves. Some women do it for power, the sense of being close to the top and perhaps privy to confidential information. For the men, it is an easy, convenient arrangement. A girl who interests them in the board room may begin to interest them in the bedroom, too.

Finding a hideaway for discreet get-togethers is difficult and usually heightens the drama of the relationship. More than a couple of magazine editors we know always required the decorators install a comfortable couch in their offices for quick trysts during supposed dictation sessions or on overtime on Saturdays. Not too long ago, many New York hotels obligingly started offering rooms by the half-day for business meetings, thereby increasing

MONEY, EGO, POWER

their hot pillow traffic during long lunch hours. But large hotel lobbies are often the scene of unexpected confrontations, so many executives prefer to take their ladies to handy motels, often located on the way to the nearest airport. Borrowing the apartment of a friend for a lunchtime picnic can be an easy solution. If the girl is single or divorced and lives alone, the problem is more easily solved, but watch out for the suspicious eyes of doormen and neighbors who might recognize the man in the elevator as the same man whose photograph appears in the business pages.

The best advice to anyone contemplating sex in the office is: don't. It is uncomfortable, time-consuming and dangerous. But, if you must, then do it on your own time. And for women in an office—if a man suggests a meeting in the supply room or a quickie in the cleaning lady's store closet, then dump him in the nearest wastebasket. He has no style, and you will be wasting your time on someone who'll never make it to the top.

Staying in Shape

The physical and mental stress on the wheeler-dealer has him very concerned with his health. Staying in good health is important, not only to give you the strength to get to the top but also to enable you to live long enough to enjoy the rewards of having got there.

Fear of heart attacks, high cholesterol counts and flabby middles have made the majority of executives hyperconscious of diet. It isn't necessary to become manic

Life Style

about food like the late Charles Revson, who ate everything charcoal-broiled to a crisp, but it is no longer just the longing-to-be-skinnier ladies who fill the waiting rooms of the cities' increasingly popular diet doctors. Thanks to doctors like Robert Atkins, Josue Corcos and Morton Glenn, more and more men are weighing in weekly with their doctors, consulting calorie and/or carbohydrate counters at restaurant business lunches and ordering their chefs to weigh their portions on postage scales, in a scientific effort to avoid a coronary, lower their cholesterol count and stay trim. It seems that many of them have given up on Dr. Stillman's water diet, since all those trips to the bathroom were taking their toll in office efficiency. Smoking, too, is on the wane, with more and more executives opting for a good cigar—not inhaled, of course—instead of their usual two packs a day.

If your ego is bruised or you find himself prone to fits of depression or feelings of failure, remember that a psychiatrist's bills are tax-deductible. At the upper levels, many executive health insurance policies cover psychiatric bills. Furthermore, a lunch hour spent at the analyst's instead of at "21" can save your figure as well as your psyche.

10

Your Future

To stay where you are, to move forward or to get out of the game altogether—that is the question. If circumstances dictate a particular course of action, then the decision might be a relatively simple one. If not, then a lot of heart-searching is required.

In August 1975, *Dun's Review,* a financial magazine, ran a series of articles called "Where Are They Now?", which sought to find out what had happened to a number of businessmen—among whom Robert Kenmore, Gerry Tsai and I could be labeled wheeler-dealers—who had had particularly high profiles during the go-go days of the 1960s. The three of us have much lower profiles these days, but for completely different reasons.

Your Future

Robert Kenmore

In the case of Robert Kenmore, formerly chief executive officer of the Kenton Corporation, the decision to get out of the big leagues was virtually made for him by the near-bankruptcy of his company.

In 1968, having given up his job as vice-president of acquisitions analysis at ITT, he gained control, first, of a company called Family Bargain Centers and then of ten more businesses, each with a glamorous name and a small base of operation, like Cartier, Ben Kahn Furs, Kenneth Jay Lane—all in the luxury category. His plan was to capitalize on the cachet those names carried with them and exploit them much more widely than they had been exploited before, by retailing their products through new distribution channels. Cartier jewelry, for example, would be sold in stores throughout the United States, not just in the Fifth Avenue store.

But by 1971 things were going badly for Kenmore and his company was reporting heavy losses. In the following year, as things got progressively worse, Kenmore resigned and sold his interest in the company to Meshulam Riklis, whose retailing empire had been so successful in the 1960s and who is the kind of wheeler-dealer who is never content to stay where he is. So, while Robert Kenmore got out of the game, Riklis not only stayed in but, again, moved ahead.

MONEY, EGO, POWER

Gerry Tsai

Gerry Tsai is a different proposition altogether. During the late 1960s, Tsai was riding the crest of the wave with his then revolutionary idea of concentrating portfolios in a small number of "growth" stocks, and of moving in and out of investments—fast. His reputation as a champion stock-selector lured an unprecedented $250 million into the Manhattan Fund, which he founded in 1966.

But the Manhattan Fund did not perform the miracles the investors had hoped for, and Tsai, seeing the handwriting on the wall, decided to get out while the getting was still reasonably good. He sold out to CNA, the Chicago insurance company, collecting some $30 million for himself. He left CNA in 1973 and came back to Wall Street with a much smaller, less glamorous operation—the brokerage house of G. Tsai and Company. Tsai may well deny it, but the way it looks is that he tried the big leagues, found them too tough and so decided to retrench.

Moving from a small area of operation to a larger one is not merely a question of scale. It requires a different set of techniques, and Tsai obviously found that the challenge of a large-scale operation was not what he wanted. To succeed in that kind of operation demands nerves of steel, stamina, guts and the sort of drive to keep achieving that Riklis has; else the damage to the man can be irreparable. Perhaps Tsai had already achieved what he set out to do. If his primary desire was to make a lot of money, then he succeeded brilliantly—$30 million is a lot of money, by any standards—and the idea of going on to run a small brokerage house where he could keep his hand in and conserve his capital makes a lot of sense. Having achieved that prime goal, he didn't have to have new mountains to climb or the stimulus of overdue bank loans needing refinancing to keep him buzzing, like Riklis.

The Quiet Life and a Final Warning

Settling for the contentment of a quiet life is a very attractive option which pays its own kind of dividend—more time to spend with your family and to do all those things you never had time for before. At least, I have found that to be true, and for me the decision about my future was easy—get out. By the end of the 1960s, I had done all the ego-tripping that wheeling and dealing in the United States during that period provided; I'd got it out of my system and I'm glad that I had. Now, at forty-four, with plenty of time left to enjoy the results of my labors, I have repaired to England and the genteel life of a lawyer once again, and of an art patron. So I no longer qualify for the "flamboyant" label hung on me during the 1960s by the *Wall Street Journal* and other papers. I have had my fill of the hassles involved in public companies and of the structured life that running a large corporation imposes. And, anyway, times have changed. These days, you make much more money with a small private company and the minimum number of employees than you can by playing the stock market.

But if you have been actively involved in the business

world for a large proportion of your adult life, and are accustomed to living under pressure, always on the brink of disaster, it may prove more difficult than you think suddenly to switch wavelengths and tune in to peace and tranquillity. Machismo—the need to prove themselves—looms large in many men's thinking. Like the insecure cocksman who is unable to pass up the chance of adding another notch to his bedstead, some men have a real need constantly to prove themselves in the business field. These are the men who are constantly jumping into new deals—and/or new beds—in an effort to convince themselves, not other people, of how successful and virile they are.

Getting out of the game is not simply the coward's way out. It takes considerable inner resources and guts. You need to be able to busy yourself with other work and activities that will give you the same degree and quality of satisfaction that you once derived from pulling off a deal or turning a profit. The transition from wheeler-dealer to private person is a difficult one and requires a kind of soul-searching that eventually enables a man to know himself. It would be pretentious to call it a mystical experience, but the sudden availability of time in which to reflect on the past, and the psychological motivations that caused it to turn out the way it did, can provide you with a rare insight into business, as well as into yourself, which would improve your ability to wheel and deal if you ever decided to return to the fray. Deciding about your future requires a basic appraisal of all the risks—and rewards—involved, and weighing all the alternatives

Your Future

in terms of your own needs and desires should yield the right answer for you.

When all is said and done, making it to the top as a wheeler-dealer is not simply a question of knowing how, or of being presented with the opportunities, or even of wanting it badly enough. It has to do more, perhaps, with being able to keep a toehold on reality, no matter how high you may be attempting to fly. Any wheeler-dealer who has got to the top and *stayed* there, has maintained that toehold—Larry Tisch, for example —whereas a man like Robert J. Ringer (author of *Winning Through Inflation*, which was on the best-seller list for months during 1975 and 1976), who had so much going for him, amounted to nothing because he lacked that vital grip on reality.

Robert Ringer was in no doubt about what went into making money—drive, ambition and, above all, the willingness to take chances. And he had all three in abundance. His climb from poor boy in Ohio to star of the Beverly Hills Bistro set began when he bootstrapped himself, with virtually no money of his own, into the presidency of Illustrated World Encyclopedia, an excellent little company on the American Stock Exchange. With the help of Clyde Skeen, former president of Jimmy Ling's L.T.V., Ringer gained control of a company with a substantial amount of cash, a small but sound publishing business, with excellent prospects.

In his meteoric rise to the top, Ringer had been given much of the advice offered in this book. All he was left with was the first draft of what became *Winning Through*

Intimidation, which has probably made him solvent again, if nothing else.

Ringer's basic problem seems to have been the failure to realize that it takes a successful, well-run company to provide all the trappings of success—the Lear jet, the tables at Le Bistro and so on. All his energies and whatever talents he had were channeled into securing and enjoying the latter, while the former was allowed to go hang. Ringer, in other words, was so busy eating the golden eggs that he allowed the goose that laid them to starve to death.

These days, such a philosophy is only half true for Robert Ringer, and only half true for Larry Tisch. Personally, he is anything but flamboyant, and his life style is extremely conservative. After thirteen years in the hotel business, Larry Tisch moved into movie theaters in 1960, when he bought Loew's. Whether it was the lure of the movies that attracted him, or merely the real estate, Loew's, with its under-utilized assets, was his jumping-off point into the big time.

While he was turning Loew's around, by selling off the unprofitable theaters and spending between $5 and $6 million to renovate others, he was also continuing to expand his hotel operations. Between 1961 and 1968, he built the Summit, the Regency and the Americana in New York City, as well as three motels, and later acquired and renovated the Drake and the Warwick in New York, the two Ambassadors in Chicago, and the Mark Hopkins in San Francisco, which was later sold off.

Now, following his move into CNA in November 1974,

Your Future

Tisch is no longer merely a wheeler-dealer. He has made the seemingly impossible transition to becoming one of the most respected, establishment businessmen in the United States.